The

Bilderberg

Group

Facts & Fiction

The

Bilderberg
Group

Facts & Fiction

Mark Dice

The Resistance
San Diego, CA

Table of Contents

Also by Mark Dice:

-*Inside the Illuminati*
-*The Illuminati: Facts & Fiction*
-*The New World Order: Facts & Fiction*
-*Illuminati in the Music Industry*
-*The Resistance Manifesto*
-*Big Brother: The Orwellian Nightmare Come True*

Connect with Mark on:

Facebook.com/MarkDice
Twitter.com/MarkDice
Instagram.com/MarkDice
YouTube.com/MarkDice
MarkDice.com

Introduction

Every spring since 1954 an elite group of around one hundred of the world's most powerful politicians, businessmen, bankers, media executives, and international royalty have been quietly gathering for a secret meeting in an evacuated five-star hotel while being protected by armed guards who stand watch. Inside, for three days, the attendees engage in lengthy off-the-record talks about the top issues facing the world. They're called the Bilderberg Group, or often just "Bilderberg" for short, and for over a half century there wasn't much more than a peep about the meeting in the American mainstream media.

For decades, many people believed this meeting was an urban legend, but as you will soon see, it is very real and very well documented. Rumors about the Bilderberg Group do seem like something out of a Hollywood movie with the cliché claims of a "secret meeting" of a group of wealthy men trying to "take over the world," but "as crazy as it sounds," in recent years a lot of allegations about the Bilderberg Group that had floated around on the Internet began to surface in some mainstream publications. To many people's surprise, such a meeting exists, and the "rumors" were true.

Between 100 to 120 of the world's top politicians, businessmen, financial fat cats, military leaders, heads of intelligence agencies, reporters, and executives from major media outlets fly half way around the world to gather once a year in the end of May or early June in a closed down fancy hotel for three days and are protected by private security contractors and local police who stand watch outside to prevent any uninvited guests from dropping by. Temporary security fences are even set up to prevent anyone from stepping foot on the property, and attempt to block the view from any onlookers who are watching from across the street to see who shows up.

The attendees arrive one after the other in tinted Lincoln Town Cars driven by professional drivers. Independent journalists and photographers have been able to discover the time and place for many of these meetings in recent years and have gotten clear photographs of some of the men and women who have attended, but most still refuse to even acknowledge they know anything about it.

Some people refer to them as "the 1%" but this label is far from accurate if you do the math. One percent of the earth's seven billion people is *70 million* people! Bilderberg is more like the .

00001% which is approximately 700 people, a figure that accounts for the steering committee and the regular attendees over the past few decades.

The meeting is named after the Bilderberg Hotel located in Oosterbeck, Holland, which was the site of their first gathering organized by Prince Bernhard of the Netherlands in 1954. Then, and still today, attendees agree not to discuss publicly who was in attendance or what specifically was discussed, and (until recently at least) most of them have denied any knowledge of the Bilderberg Group at all when—on the rare occasion—someone asked them about it—usually a citizen journalist or YouTuber.

For decades, news of the shadowy Bilderberg Group spread in so-called "anti-government" Patriot circles, in underground newsletters, and "conspiracy" websites, until the advent of YouTube and social media finally forced *some* major mainstream media outlets to admit that Bilderberg is real and some very powerful people attend. After these decades of news blackouts, with the rise of social media and video sharing sites like YouTube, slowly more and more major news outlets have begun to at least mention the Bilderberg Group, albeit ever so briefly, and usually including the caveat that "conspiracy theorists" are upset or "paranoid" about them. Through the increase in popularity of alternative news websites and the emergence of social media, more and more people began learning about this strange and secretive meeting, and it got to a point where mainstream outlets basically had to at least mention it was happening in attempts to avoid looking like they were covering it up by purposefully avoiding the issue.[1]

For years, if anyone called into any of the major syndicated talk radio shows like Rush Limbaugh, Sean Hannity, Glenn Beck and others, and told the call screener they wanted to ask about the Bilderberg Group, that person's call would never be put through. "We're not taking calls on that right now, sorry. Click." If the person calling gave the call screener a bogus question and happened to be put on air and then asked the host about the Bilderbergers, they would be ridiculed and the call would be dropped immediately (something that's happened to me many times).[2]

Why not take it seriously? Why pretend for so many years they don't exist? Are these radio talk

---

[1] *Time Magazine* "Bilderberg: The Uber-Powerful Global Elite Meet Behind Closed Doors in St. Moritz" by Anne Fournier (June 9th 2011)

[2] Many of these calls were recorded or the clips were taken from the show's podcast archive and can be heard on MarkDice.com or found on YouTube if you search for keywords: Mark Dice Bilderberg Sean Hannity.

show hosts and other major news editors and reporters "in on it?" Has there been a "conspiracy" to keep the meeting out of the press? It's foolish to deny that there hasn't been an arrangement between the Bilderberg Group and the American mainstream media to keep them out of the news and to have the top political analysts and talk show hosts pretend like they don't know anything about them all these years. When 100 of the world's most influential politicians, media owners, banking executives, and business elite fly half way around the world to meet for three days in a closed down luxury hotel that's fenced off and surrounded by armed guards, nobody can say that's not a newsworthy or interesting event!

Critics see this small, tightly knit group as an Aristocracy or an Oligarchy, comprised of men (and some women) who see themselves as having the right to rule because of their wealth and "superior intelligence" who put their own interests above anyone else's—with little to no regard for the consequences. Without the proper checks and balances put in place, which was the intention of the Founding Fathers when they split the government into three different branches (Executive, Judicial, and Legislative) in what's called the separation of powers, a government can become so powerful it is difficult to oppose them when their actions are unfair or illegal. And when their discussions aren't open to public scrutiny it makes keeping them in check even more difficult.

Many people believe that this meeting is possibly a violation of the Logan Act, which prohibits unauthorized citizens from negotiating with foreign governments, a law that was implemented to prevent people from interfering with international relations between the United States and other countries. It specifically states, "Any citizen of the United States, wherever he may be, who, without authority of the United States, directly or indirectly commences or carries on any correspondence or intercourse with any foreign government or any officer or agent thereof, with intent to influence the measures or conduct of any foreign government or of any officer or agent thereof, in relation to any disputes or controversies with the United States, or to defeat the measures of the United States, shall be fined under this title or imprisoned not more than three years, or both."

Is the Bilderberg Group negotiating foreign policy? Is this where the ruling elite come to a consensus to guide the direction of the world in their favor? Or is it simply "just another conference?" Or, are the "conspiracy theorists" right? What is the evidence? How were they first discovered? What are they doing? And should the public be concerned? Do they choose who the next president of the United States will be? Do they covertly coordinate economic booms and busts?

Do they manipulate foreign policy and decide which wars will be launched and when from behind these closed doors? Is this annual meeting of the power elite really just not interesting or newsworthy? Has there been a cover-up or a conspiracy to keep them out of the headlines? Why the secrecy and the denials for so many years? Is this the "shadow government?" Those questions and more will be answered in *The Bilderberg Group: Facts & Fiction.*

THE MARRIOTT HOTEL IN CHANTILLY, VIRGINIA
PROTECTED BY A TEMPORARY PRIVACY AND
SECURITY FENCE SET UP FOR THE 2012 MEETING.

PROTESTERS TRYING TO IDENTIFY THE ATTENDEES
AS THEY ARRIVE FOR THE 2012 MEETING IN
CHANTILLY, VIRGINIA.

The Attendees

Each year the list of attendees reads like a who's who of the ruling class. Just a small sample of some of the people who attend are: David Rockefeller and Henry Kissinger, who have both been regular attendees for decades (and helped finance the group as is shown on their tax returns); banking bigwigs like the CEOs or chairmen from Goldman Sachs, Citigroup, HSBC, Deutsche Bank, JP Morgan Chase, American Express, etc; not to mention the head and former head of the Federal Reserve Bank like Ben Bernanke and Alan Greenspan, as well as U.S. Treasury secretary Timothy Geithner and other international financial fat cats like the head of the World Bank and the IMF.[3]

In the tech world we've seen Microsoft founder Bill Gates, Google's Executive Chairman Eric Schmidt;[4] Jeff Bezos CEO of Amazon.com

---

[3] http://www.bilderbergmeetings.org/participants_2008.html

[4] *The Guardian* "Bilderberg conference 2014: eating our politicians for breakfast" by Charlie Skelton (May 30th 2014)

(just before buying the Washington Post in 2013);[5] Louis Gerstner the CEO of IBM; Peter Thiel, founder of Pay Pal and major investor in Facebook; as well as Chris Hughes, the co-founder of Facebook and other tech titans all attend.

Over the years leading media figures such as the publisher of the *Washington Post*, as well as the chief editors of the *New York Times*, *Los Angeles Times*, the *Wall Street Journal*, *Time*, *Newsweek*, and other major newspapers and magazines have all attended or regularly attend. Executives from the top television networks like News Corp CEO Rupert Murdoch and representatives from ABC, NBC, and CBS are also key fixtures, as well as popular political commentators and reporters.

Top military brass and U.S. intelligence figures like David Petraeus (former head of the CIA), General Michael Haden (former NSA chief), General Keith Alexander (current head of the NSA);[6] Donald Rumsfeld, former Secretary of Defense and one of the architects of the Iraq War; General Colin Powell; NATO's Secretary General,

---

[5] *Business Insider* "The Full List Of Incredibly Powerful People Who Will Attend This Year's Bilderberg Meeting (June 3rd 2013)

[6] http://www.bilderbergmeetings.org/participants2012.html

the head of Britain's Secret Service; and others are also regular attendees.

Top American politicians like Secretary of State John Kerry, Senators John Edwards, Tom Daschele, Chuck Hagel, Hillary Clinton have all attended; as well as members of British Parliament and European royalty. Even Presidents Clinton and Ford (before they were elected). No seated president ever attends because their schedule and whereabouts is so closely monitored they couldn't risk brining so much attention to the event.

Could all these globalist movers and shakers be getting together just to have coffee and hang out? Or, as many believe, could this think tank be a place where an elite consensus is arrived about how to best maintain and expand their power and influence?

The British newspaper *The Observer* (sister paper to *The Guardian*) surprisingly ran an article back in 1963 that remarked, "These people [Bilderbergers] maintain that the future belongs to technocrats, because the rumor among them is that the grave questions of international affairs are too delicate to be left in the hands of diplomats. However, the 'clandestiny' of their debates shows that they only seek one thing: effective domination over the peoples of the world, but by dissimulating [concealing] themselves and by leaving the responsibility of the governments in the hands of petty politicians."[7]

PROTESTERS TRYING TO GET A PHOTO OF WHO IS ARRIVING IN THE BACK OF THIS TINTED LINCOLN TOWN CAR AT 2012 BILDERBERG MEETING.

---

[7] *The Observer* April 7th 1963

Recent Meetings

The conference is held in various countries throughout Europe at luxury hotels and usually every fourth year it returns to the United States—on election years, which is no coincidence—often meeting in Chantilly, Virginia which is just a short drive outside Washington D.C. This makes it convenient for politicians and the Eastern Establishment in New York City to attend without drawing too much suspicion since they don't have to leave the country and create a cover story for their prolonged absence.

The entire hotel is cleared out around noon the day before the meeting and no reservations are accepted during this time so only Bilderberg members and guests are allowed in the hotel. Actually—to be more specific—only members and guests are allowed on the property since barricades and temporary fences are set up and local police and private security teams patrol the perimeter and guard the entrances.

The hotels which are chosen are secluded on large plots of land, and never downtown in a major city. This makes it easier for members and guests to arrive without being identified. If the meeting were held at a hotel in downtown

Manhattan for example, onlookers could easily hang out on the side walk or across the street to catch a glimpse (or take photos or video) of the attendees coming or going. It is for this reason the location is always at a resort-style hotel with plenty of land, hidden away from nearby streets and neighboring buildings.

The hotel staff is also sworn to secrecy and may likely be coerced into signing non-disclosure agreements to prevent them from talking to the press (and the protesters). When I was at the Marriott in Chantilly, Virginia the day before it was cleared out for the 2012 Bilderberg meeting, I asked the bar tender if he knew what was about to happen over the next few days and he said he couldn't talk about it.

There is a core group of regulars, many of whom have been involved for decades. A steering committee decides who is invited and what topics will be disguised. Each day's meeting is broken up into two sessions in the morning and two sessions in the afternoon, except the final day which only has the two morning sessions. A different topic is discussed during each session. Some recent meeting locations and dates are as follows:

- 2015 Telfs, Austria (June 11th - June 14th) at the Interalpen hotel.

- 2014 Copenhagen, Denmark (May 29th - June 1st) at the Marriott hotel.

- 2013 Watford, United Kingdom (June 6th - 9th) at the Grove Hotel.

- 2012 Chantilly, Virginia, USA (May 31st - June 3rd) at Westfields Marriott hotel.

- 2011 St. Moritz, Switzerland (June 9th - 12th) at the Suvretta House.

- 2010 Sitges, Spain (June 3rd - 6th) at the Hotel Dolce.

- 2009 Vouliagmeni, Greece (May 14th - 17th) at the Astir Palace resort.

- 2008 Chantilly, Virginia, USA (June 5th - 8th) at the Westfields Marriott.

- 2007 Istanbul, Turkey (May 31st - June 3rd) at the Ritz-Carlton Hotel in Sisli.

- 2006 Ottawa, Ontario, Canada (June 8th - 11th) at the Brookstreet Hotel in Kanata.

- 2005 Rottach-Egern, Germany (May 5th - 8th) at the Dorint Sofitel Seehotel Überfahrt.

**A FEW HUNDRED PROTESTERS SHOW THEIR
DISAPPROVAL OF BILDERBERG 2012**

How Were They First Discovered?

In 1957 a Pulitzer Prize winning columnist named Westbrook Pegler who wrote for *Scripps Howard News Service*, the *Chicago Tribune*, and other papers, published the first article on the Bilderberg Group—although he didn't know their name at the time—his report marked the beginning of the unraveling of one of the most interesting "conspiracy theories" of all time.

Pegler wrote, "Something very mysterious is going on when a strange assortment of 67 self-qualified, polyglot [bilingual] designers and arbiters of the economic and political fate of our western world go into a secret huddle on an island of Brunswick, GA and not a word gets into the popular press beyond a little routine AP story. These gumshoe super state architects and monetary schemers were drawn from all NATO countries. The fact of this weird conclave as spooky as any midnight meeting of the Ku Klux Klan in a piney woods, was bound to get known to the world eventually."[8]

---

[8] Tucker, Jim – *Jim Tucker's Bilderberg Diary* page 231

He continued to explain how he first learned of this meeting, saying, "I got my first word of it from a reader who happened onto St. Simon Island, Brunswick, [Georgia] on her way to West Palm Beach. She wrote that the hotel on St. Simon was almost deserted, but that when she commented on this, the clerk said the place had been alive with mysterious characters a few days earlier and with Secret Service and FBI too."

While not yet knowing their name, Westbrook did see similarities between this meeting and the secret Jekyll Island meeting that was held in 1910 by a small group of America's elite where they discussed and drew up plans for the Federal Reserve Banking System. He said, "Senator Aldrich of Rhode Island, called this one into being. He was the father of Winthrop Aldrich. There have been many excited versions of that ancient hoe-down on Jekyll Island, but relatively few have ever heard of it all."

After he began criticizing executives of the powerful Hearst Corporation, which owned and controlled almost 30 different newspapers in America at the time, he was fired. Hearst newspapers literally created "yellow journalism" which refers to sensationalistic headlines and careless reporting with a disregard for the facts in order to sell more newspapers, something that has pretty much become standard practice in American mainstream media.

A man named Willis Carto read Westbrook Pegler's article about this intriguing meeting and it inspired him to begin investigating the issue himself. A year after Westbrook Pegler's article came out, Willis Carto began publishing a newsletter called *Liberty Lowdown* and would later begin publishing a newspaper called *The Spotlight* which was largely dedicated to tracking and exposing this elusive group.

Over two decades later, a reporter named Jim Ticker would learn of the Bilderberg Group when going to work for *The Spotlight.* Tucker immediately became obsessed with them, and would later become the world's foremost expert on the meeting. Tucker explained, "Had it not been for Willis A. Cato, who hired me as editor of *The Spotlight* and then put me on the tack of Bilderberg, I would probably—almost assuredly—never heard of the word 'Bilderberg.' Having had the opportunity, through Carto's good offices as founder of Liberty Lobby, publisher of *The Spotlight*, to begin what ultimately proved to be a generation of world-wide Bilderberg-hunting, I was able to bring news about Bilderberg to literally millions of folks who would like myself have otherwise remained in the dark about these globalist schemers."[9]

Tucker had somehow gained the support of an insider who would leak information to him every year about the location and date of the meeting, as well as attendee lists and other details. Tucker obsessively tracked the Bilderberg Group from 1975 until his death in 2013 at the age of 78. His book, titled *Jim Tucker's Bilderberg Diary* contains decades of information about where the Bilderbergers met, who was in attendance, and what was discussed.[10]

As Tucker's health began to fail, he turned over his trusted source (or sources) who tipped him off each year as to the meeting's location and dates, to Alex Jones from Infowars.com. Love him or hate him, Alex Jones played a large role in getting major media to finally cover the Bilderberg Group meetings in the early 2000's. In 2006 he traveled to Ottawa, Canada after being tipped off that was where they were going to meet, and Alex Jones has announced the location every year since and has been able to get a growing number of supporters (expanding from a few hundred in

---

[9] Tucker, Jim – *Jim Tucker's Bilderberg Diary* page 218

[10] The book was unfortunately out of print the last I checked, but used copies were available on amazon.com.

2012[11] to over 2000 in Hertfordshire, England in 2014) to meet outside the hotel to peacefully protest and raise awareness about the meetings.[12]

With Alex's huge audience and popular website, it became impossible for the Bilderberg Group to hide anymore, and now in the last few years they quietly admit when and where they are meeting through their simple website BilderbergMeetings.org. In 2011 the massively popular news site, the Drudge Report, first posted links to Infowars articles and some European papers which covered the event.[13] This was basically the dam bursting since the Drudge Report has a tremendous influence on what topics people talk about, and is the homepage of many reporters and political analysts in the United States.[14]

---

[11] *The Guardian* "Bilderberg 2012: protesters hail their hero, Alex Jones" Ryan Devereaux (June 3rd 2012)

[12] *NPR* "Bewildered by Bilderberg" by Linton Weeks (May 21st 2014)

[13] *The Guardian* "Bilderberg 2011: The curtains are drawn" by Charlie Skelton (June 9th 2011)

[14] *Washington Examiner* "Drudge is the nation's news homepage, top driver to Fox, NYT, Politico" by Paul Bedard (April 9th 2015)

JIM TUCKER TALKS TO A GROUP OF PROTESTERS ABOUT HIS ADVENTURES TRACKING BILDERBERG.

ALEX JONES SPEAKS TO THE PROTESTERS OUTSIDE THE 2012 BILDERBERG MEETING IN CHANTILLY, VIRGINIA.

Tax Returns

I have been able to obtain several recent years of Bilderberg's IRS filings since they are registered as a 501c3 "charitable foundation" certain financial information must be made available for public inspection—if you know where to look.[15] I discovered they operate under the business entity "American Friends of Bilderberg" and the documents show that in 2008 they received $645,000 in contributions to fund their annual meeting, with money coming from Goldman Sachs ($25,000), Microsoft ($75,000), Henry Kissinger ($20,000), David Rockefeller ($50,000) and other wealthy donors. The 2009 returns show the *Washington Post* newspaper donated $25,000.[16]

Under the "Summary of Direct Charitable Activities," the forms list the organization's goals as "Organizing & sponsoring conferences which study & discuss significant problems of the western alliance [and] collaborating on the Bilderberg meetings held in Europe & North America."

---

[15] 2008 IRS Form 990-PF OMD No 1545-0052

[16] 2009 IRS Form 990-PF OMD No 1545-0052

The expenses on the 2008 and 2012 documents (when they met in the United States) are listed as approximately $900,000 per year, which covers renting out the entire hotel for three days, paying the private security forces and compensating local police for the extra man-hours, the catering companies (or hotel restaurants) to feed them, and presumably for paying the travel expenses of members and attendees. There is most likely a European entity that functions as a counterpart to "American Friends of Bilderberg" that is used to pay the bills when the group meets in Europe because the recent forms I have been able to obtain show the expenses drop to around $100,000 per year when the group meets outside the United States, and then jump up close to one million dollars in the years they meet in the U.S.[17]

The documents list James Johnson as the treasurer, who is also the chairman of Perseus, a merchant bank and private equity fund management company based in Washington D.C. with offices in New York and an associated advisory firm in Munich, Germany.[18]   The name

---

[17] Usually they meet in the United States every four years, typically in election years, although this has not always been the case.

[18] http://www.goldmansachs.com/who-we-are/leadership/board-of-directors/james-a-johnson.html

Perseus comes from Greek Mythology and is the demigod who beheaded Medusa. James Johnson was once the Chairman of the Executive Committee at Fannie Mae [The Federal National Mortgage Association]; and before that he was a managing director at Lehman Brothers, the fourth-largest investment bank in the U.S. (which failed during the economic crisis of 2008).[19] He's also on the Board of Directors for Goldman Sachs and a member of the Council on Foreign Relations.[20]

I have personally been to the offices of Perseus in Washington D.C. seeking a comment on the documents, which I held in my hand during my visit, and as soon as I mentioned "Bilderberg," James Johnson's secretary said they have no comment, ordered me to leave, and slammed the door. A video of this encounter is posted on my YouTube channel, YouTube.com/MarkDice.[21] The person listed on the forms as the accountant is Robert T. Foldes of Leon D. Alpern & Company, and when I called them, the secretary confirmed

---

[19] *CBS News* "The Case Against Lehman Brothers" by Steve Kroft (August 19th 2012)

[20] See my previous book *Inside the Illuminati, Evidence, Objectives, and Methods of Operation* for a detailed analysis of this and other Bilderberg affiliates.

[21] YouTube: Mark Dice Visits Bilderberg's Secret Office in Washington D.C. (June 2nd 2014)

they handle the taxes for American Friends of Bilderberg but declined to give me any further information. I have published some of the financial records on MarkDice.com where you can download the PDFs if you want.[22]

---

[22] Visit MarkDice.com and then click the link to "Articles by Mark" and you'll see another link to the Bilderberg's Tax Returns listed where you can download the PDFs from several different years.

Politicians Silent

Attendees of the meeting agree to the Chatham House Rule, which is an anonymity policy created by the Royal Institute of International Affairs (nicknamed Chatham House) which is an elite think tank established in 1920 in the United Kingdom that analyzes and promotes their international political policies. The Chatham House Rule basically means that people in attendance are forbidden from discussing who attended and may not attribute any specific statements made by anyone in attendance at any time in the future. It's basically a "what happens in Vegas, stays in Vegas" kind of oath.

The rule is supposedly in place to facilitate frank and honest discussions about any controversial topics which people may not want to go on the record about due to the political or personal consequences of letting their true feelings be publicly known.

Chatham House is essentially Britain's counterpart to the Council on Foreign Relations in America, which sounds like a committee in Congress, but is in fact a private organization that serves up its political propaganda on a silver platter to the elite politicians and journalists who are members.   While some politicians will acknowledge their affiliation with the CFR— admitting anything about the Bilderberg Group is a whole other story.

Barack Obama

As Election Day in 2008 approached, then presidential candidate Barack Obama ditched the reporters traveling with him on his campaign so he could attend a secret meeting which his press secretary Robert Gibbs refused to give any information about.[23]   It just so happened the Bilderbergers were meeting at this same time. As is common during the approach of a presidential election, reporters from major media outlets travel around the country with the candidates to give continuous coverage of their every move, and in June of 2008—on the same day the Bilderberg Group was meeting in Chantilly, Virginia (about 30-40 minutes outside of Washington D.C.)— reporters found out that Obama had ditched them after they were all stuck on a flight which they were told he was scheduled to be on with them.

"Reporters traveling with Obama sensed

---

[23] YouTube: Robert Gibbs Lies to Press on CNN avoids disclosing Bilderberg Meeting https://www.youtube.com/watch?v=NIPik872K64

something might be happening between the pair [Obama and Hillary] when they arrived at Dulles International Airport after an event in Northern Virginia and Obama was not aboard the airplane," the Associated Press reported.[24] Not only was he not aboard the plane, as everyone was led to believe he would be, but his campaign literally trapped reporters on the flight so they couldn't follow him.

"Why were we not told about this meeting until we were on the plane, the doors were shut and the plane was about to taxi to take off?" one reporter asked, confronting Obama's spokesman Robert Gibbs on the flight about what had just happened. The confrontation was caught on camera by one reporter and can be seen on YouTube.[25]

Gibbs replied, "Senator Obama had a desire to do some meetings, others had a desire to meet with him tonight in a private way, and that is what we are doing."

---

[24] *Associated Press* "Clinton and Obama hold secret meeting" by Beth Fouhy and Nedra Pickler (June 5th 2008)

[25] YouTube: Robert Gibbs Lies to Press on CNN avoids disclosing Bilderberg Meeting (posted by user 911isalie on February 26th 2009)
https://www.youtube.com/watch?v=NIPik872K64

Another reporter asked, "Is there more than one meeting, is there more than one person with whom he is meeting?"

"I am not going to get into all the details of the meeting," Gibbs replied.

Of course, it's not a stretch of the imagination to assume Obama was meeting with the Bilderberg Group, who usually schedule their event within a short driving distance from Washington D.C. every election year.

Hillary Clinton

When Hillary Clinton was running for president in 2008, someone asked her about the Bilderberg Group at an event when she was at a campaign stop in New Hampshire. It was a brief encounter that happened when she was shaking hands with people in the crowd, and the person who asked her videotaped the interaction and posted it on YouTube. "What's going on at the Bilderberg meeting and what are you guys talking about up there?" he asked, in a polite and sincere tone.[26]

---

[26] YouTube: Did Hillary Clinton Attend the 2006 Bilderberg Conference? (Shot November 8th 2007) Posted on YouTube by user jamartellxiv on November 17th 2011 https://www.youtube.com/watch?v=wqbItHSPGi0

Hillary cackled, "Ha ha ha. I have no idea what you're talking about." The man responded, "Why are they such top secret meetings?" To which she answered (looking like a kid with their hand caught in the cookie jar), "Sir, I have no idea what you're talking about," and then she turned from him and walked away.[27]

How could she have no idea what he was talking about? How could one of the most politically connected and powerful women in the world not know what the Bilderberg Group is or what they do? It's ridiculous to believe that she isn't intimately aware of them and was obviously playing dumb so she wouldn't betray they them by acknowledging they exist.

After being the First Lady during her husband Bill Clinton's presidency in the 1990s, Hillary went on to become a senator in New York and then Secretary of State during Barack Obama's first term as president; and at the time I'm writing this book, is running for president again in 2016. Since her college days, she has carefully plotted her political career and has long hoped to become the first female president of the United States.

---

[27] YouTube: Did Hillary Clinton Attend the 2006 Bilderberg Conference? (Shot November 8th 2007) Posted on YouTube by user jamartellxiv on November 17th 2011 https://www.youtube.com/watch?v=wqbItHSPGi0

In 1969 she wrote her senior thesis on Saul
Alinsky, a left-wing extremist who detailed his
subversive tactics aimed at creating a New World
Order in is 1971 book *Rules for Radicals,* which
he literally dedicated to Lucifer in the foreword.
For years the Clintons were able to have the 92-
page thesis sealed, and it wasn't made public until
someone leaked it in 2007.[28]   The president of
Hillary's alma mater, Wellesley College in
Massachusetts, approved sealing the thesis at the
Clintons' request under the bizarre new rule that
any senior thesis written by a   president or first
lady of the United States would be sealed, but the
work of every other alumni was publicly available
for anyone who wanted to read them.[29]

Bill Clinton

When Bill Clinton was out campaigning for
his wife Hillary in 2008, a protester in the
audience began making a scene and shouting
about his little known meeting with Bilderberg
Group in the early 1990s causing Clinton to try to
defuse the situation by saying, "This is the deal

---

[28] *NBCNews.com* "Reading Hillary Rodham's Hidden
Thesis" by Bill Dedman (5-9-2007)

[29] Ibid.

folks, all these people that are paranoid about the world come and scream at me everywhere."[30]

The protester kept shouting him down while he tried to speak, forcing Bill to plead with him since security hadn't yet been able to reach the man in the middle of the crowd to usher him out. "You said you would go if I answered the question right? All right here's the answer. I happened to be in Europe then on my way to Russia, I was invited to go to Bilderberg by Vernon Jordan, a friend of mine, and a genuine hero of the civil rights movement. And to the best of my knowledge, NAFTA was not discussed by anybody in my presence. I was talking to people from Europe who did not give a rip about NAFTA. Now goodbye. Thank you."[31]

According to leaks, NAFTA—the North American Free Trade Agreement, was a Bilderberg idea and they were instrumental in getting the treaty drafted, which was signed into law by Bill Clinton in 1993, merging Canada, the United States and Mexico into one trilateral trading bloc, reducing or eliminating tariffs and other trade barriers.

---

[30] YouTube "Bill Clinton admits to attending 1991 Bilderberg Meeting" (March 2008)

[31] Ibid.

Before attending Bilderberg in 1991, Bill Clinton was a virtually unheard of governor of the small and little noticed state of Arkansas, but those in the Establishment caught notice of his silver tongue and his lust for power and thought he would be the perfect puppet to promote their policies as president. They don't call him "Slick Willie" for nothing. Bill Clinton's ability to lie convincingly and cleverly use vague language to avoid painting himself in a corner is unmatched by most politicians.

At a different Hillary 2008 campaign event when Bill Clinton was speaking, another heckler began shouting at him, this time about the Bohemian Grove—a less formal, sort of Bilderberg camping trip and secret elite men's retreat held every summer. Once again, trying to appease the protester who completely derailed his speech, Clinton responded, "The Bohemian Club? Did you say Bohemian Club? That's where all those rich Republicans go up and stand naked against redwood trees right? I've never been to the Bohemian Club but you ought to go. It'd be good for you. You'd get some fresh air."[32]

---

[32] YouTube "Bill Clinton gets asked about the Bohemian Grove club that he and other elites attend" (uploaded October 2011)

His comment about Republicans "standing naked against redwood trees" refers to the common practice of Bohemian Grove members openly urinating on the side of trees or in the bushes while hanging out deep within the club's 2700-acre redwood forest in Northern California where the world's most wealthy and well-to-do men meet for a private party every July.[33]

Video of Clinton's confrontation is on YouTube if you'd like to see it, and if you're not familiar with the Bohemian Grove or would like to read an in depth analysis of this truly bizarre "Bilderberg in the woods," I encourage you to pick up my book *Inside the Illuminati: Evidence, Objectives, and Methods of Operation* in paperback from Amazon.com or download it onto your tablet or e-reader from any major e-book store.

Senator Barbara Boxer

In June 2012 just one day after the Bilderberg meeting came to a close that year, my friend Luke Rudkowski, a YouTube producer and founder of We Are Change, happened to spot California

---

[33] See the section on the Bohemian Grove in my previous book *Inside the Illuminati: Evidence, Objectives, and Methods of Operation.*

Senator Barbara Boxer inside the Hart Senate Office Building in Washington D.C. in the press area giving an interview. Of course we took the opportunity to try to get a statement from her on Bilderberg as soon as her interview was over. A video of this confrontation is available on YouTube.[34]

Both Luke and I walked up to her with our professional-looking handheld wireless microphones as she was making her way down the hall and asked in a polite tone, "What are your thoughts on the important Bilderberg meeting that happened this weekend?" She immediately turned to one of her assistants who was with her and said, "Zack, do you want to make a statement?"

Boxer's Assistant: "Sure. Why don't you just give us a call (handing me his business card) and we'd be happy to get you a statement."

Me: "We'd like your statement right now. The Bilderberg meeting happened and [there was] no major media or press coverage. Just one statement about the Bilderberg meeting."

---

[34] YouTube: Senator Boxer Confronted on Bilderberg Group by Mark Dice and Luke Rudkowski from We Are Change (posted June 6th 2012)

At this point she enters an elevator and when I tried to follower her inside, her aid blocked me and she said it was for "Senators only."

Me: "Why no comment on the Bilderberg meeting?"

Boxer: "Do your job and call my office."

Me: "Do your job and answer a question please."

As the door is closing she says "Thank you very much. Thank you so much." Luke Rudkowski kept holding the door, causing it to retreat back into the wall for a few seconds and preventing the elevator from moving.

I continued to press her. "The Bilderberg meeting just happened this year…"

Boxer: "Thank you so much. I appreciate it. Just call the office. Thanks a lot."

At this point, one of her two aids exited the elevator to block us and prevent Luke from holding the door open any longer, and then it finally closed and she escaped. I did call her office just like her assistant asked, and left a message, but nobody ever called me back. Go figure.

Ben Bernanke

Independent journalist Luke Rudkowski, who has confronted countless powerful politicians on a variety of issues using his own unique style of ambush journalism, once asked Federal Reserve Chairman Ben Bernanke face to face for a comment on Bilderberg at a black tie event in New York City, but Bernanke refused and turned away.[35]

Luke: "Hey Ben, just really quick. What did you do at the 2008 Bilderberg meeting?"

Ben: "I'm not doing any press today."

Luke: [Repeating his question again] "I mean what did you do at the Bilderberg Group?"

Ben: "I'm not doing any press today." [turns away]

---

[35] YouTube: Ben Bernanke Confronted by WeAreChange (posted May 13th 2011) https://www.youtube.com/watch?v=4AcpznV4RGY

David Rockefeller

One quote floating around the Internet attributed to David Rockefeller senior, a longtime Bilderberg attendee and financier, is, "We are grateful to *The Washington Post, The New York Times, Time* magazine and other great publications whose directors have attended our meetings and respected their promises of discretion for almost forty years. ... It would have been impossible for us to develop our plan for the world if we had been subject to the bright lights of publicity during those years. But, the world is now much more sophisticated and prepared to march towards a world government. The supranational sovereignty of an intellectual elite and world bankers is surely preferable to the national auto-determination practiced in past centuries."[36]

He allegedly made this statement at the Bilderberg meeting in Baden-Baden Germany in 1991 and the comments were printed in several right-wing French newspapers but its authenticity is uncertain and disputed.

What is not disputed, however, is David Rockefeller's admission in his own memoir which he published in 2003, that, "For more than a century, ideological extremists at either end of the

---

[36] This quote is unverified and its authenticity is disputed.

political spectrum have seized upon well-publicized incidents such as my encounter with Castro to attack the Rockefeller family for the inordinate influence they claim we wield over American political and economic institutions. Some even believe we are part of a secret cabal working against the best interests of the United States, characterizing my family and me as 'internationalists' and of conspiring with others around the world to build a more integrated global political and economic structure — one world, if you will. If that is the charge, I stand guilty, and I am proud of it."[37]

Dick Cheney

When giving a speech in 2002 at Bilderberg's sister society, the Council on Foreign Relations, Vice President Dick Cheney cracked an inside joke about his membership, saying "I want to thank you all for the warm welcome today. I see a lot of old friends in the room. And it's good to be back at the Council on Foreign Relations. As Pete mentioned, I've been a member for a long time, and was actually a director for some period of time. I never mentioned that when I was

---

[37] Rockefeller, David - *Memoirs* page 405

campaigning for reelection back home in Wyoming (laughter) but it stood me in good stead. I value very much my experience, exposure to the tremendous people involved and the involvement and the ideas and the debates on the great policy issues of the day."[38]

He never mentioned his membership when campaigning because he—and everyone else in the audience—knows very well the sinister reputation the CFR has. Everyone laughed because they "got" why he never mentioned it. Despite masquerading as if it were just another benign committee in Congress and trying to hide in plain sight, Dick Cheney's joke shows that they have not been able to fool everyone about the nature of their activities. This is the same organization that Hillary Clinton once admitted she goes to in order to be "told what we should be doing and how we should think about the future."[39]

The CFR was founded in 1921 by Woodrow Wilson's chief advisor Colonel Edward Mandell House; along with Paul Warburg, who was at the

---

[38] CFR.org "Launch of the Maurice R. Greenberg Center for Geoeconomic Studies with Vice President Dick Cheney" (February 15th 2002)

[39] YouTube "Hillary Clinton addresses the Council on Foreign Relations, admits CFR runs the government

secret Jekyll Island meeting in 1910 which gave birth to the Federal Reserve Bank; Elihu Root, who was the Secretary of War under both President McKinley and Roosevelt; and a handful of other elitists who then received funding for their venture from the Rockefeller family.

Ron Paul

Congressman Ron Paul is one of the rare honest politicians who never sugar coated his statements and never shied away from criticizing his own party when he felt their actions were going against their principles throughout his 23 years as a Congressman from Texas.

At a book signing in 2008 he was once asked about the Bilderberg Group by a fan who videotaped the interaction and posted it on YouTube. "Did you hear about that recent Bilderberg Group meeting in Chantilly, Virginia?" the person asked.[40]

Ron Paul responded, "Yeah, recently there was one and there were some reports on it—I didn't

---

[40] YouTube: "Ron Paul talks about the Bilderberg Group" (posted August 16th 2008) https://www.youtube.com/watch?v=plo-1rLZ3Jo

read a whole lot about it, but they certainly were there."[41]

The person then asked what he thought they were doing, and Ron Paul responded, "Well, they probably get together and talk about how they're going to control the banking systems of the world and natural resources—and we get together and talk about how we're going to get our freedom back. So we have our own things to talk about too."[42]

Ron Paul didn't play dumb by pretending he didn't know what the guy was talking about, and he didn't laugh off his question either—instead, he answered it quite frankly, which is surprising for a politician, especially when it comes to talking about the infamous Bilderberg Group. Ron Paul (and his son Rand) are (and still may be, depending on what happens after this book is published) the only politicians in the last forty years (at the time I'm writing this) to have ever even uttered the word "Bilderberg," and to have answered people's questions in a serious manor is quite commendable. It's possible that with awareness of the Bilderberg Group spreading,

---

[41] YouTube: "Ron Paul talks about the Bilderberg Group" (posted August 16th 2008) https://www.youtube.com/watch?v=plo-1rLZ3Jo

[42] Ibid.

more politicians may seriously address the issue when asked, since it's almost impossible to pretend they don't know about it at this point in time.

Rand Paul

Luke Rudkowski from the YouTube channel We Are Change asked Kentucky Senator and 2016 Presidential Candidate Rand Paul (son of Ron Paul) about the Bilderberg Group in 2012, and just like his father, instead of ducking the question, he answered it quite candidly.[43]

Luke: "Our organization confronted [Federal Reserve Chairman] Ben Bernanke on his ties with the Bilderberg Group. Do you know anything about the Bilderberg Group?"

Rand: "Only what I've learned from Alex Jones."

Luke: "For the people who don't know what's going on can you tell people who are the

---

[43] YouTube: Rand Paul before endorsing Romney on Bilderberg and Goldman Sachs posted by WeAreChange (June 8th 2012) Interview with Rand Paul by Luke Rudkowski.

Bilderberg Group, if you feel comfortable doing so?"

Rand: "I'm not probably the world's expert on it, but I think it's people who get together who are very wealthy people who I think manipulate and use government for their own personal advantage. And I think that's the biggest thing that would help us combat this, is that they want to make this out like they're just out to help humanity and world government will be good for humanity, but guess what? World government is good for their pocketbook. They're very wealthy and they use government to make more money for themselves and that's where you expose them."

John Rarick

In 1971 a member of the U.S. House of Representatives from Louisiana named John Rarick somehow heard about these meetings and became suspicious. He wanted to know if tax dollars were being used to pay for American officials to attend. John Rarick typed up a ten-page statement and actually entered it into the official Congressional Record.

His statement begins, "Mr. Speaker, on several occasions during recent months, I called the attention of our colleagues to activities of the Bilderbergers—an elite international group comprised of high government officials, international financiers, businessmen, and opinion-makers..."

"This exclusive international aristocracy holds highly secret meetings annually or more often in various countries. The limited information available about what transpires at these meetings reveals that they discuss matters of vital importance which affect the lives of all citizens. Presidential Advisor Henry Kissinger, who made a secret visit to Peking from July 9 to July 11, 1971, and arranged for a presidential visit to Red China, was reported to be in attendance at the most recent Bilderberg meeting held in Woodstock, Vermont, April 23 to April 25, 1971. The two points reportedly discussed at the Woodstock meeting were, 'the contribution of business in dealing with current problems of social instability' and 'the possibility of a change of the American role in the world and its consequences.'"

He continues, "Following these secret discussions, which are certainly not in keeping with the Western political tradition of 'open covenants openly arrived at,' the participants returned to their respective countries with the general public left uninformed, notwithstanding the attendance of some news media representatives, of any of the recommendations and plans agreed upon as a result of the discussions—or for that matter even the occurrence of the meeting itself."[44]

Since Rarick's statements in 1971, to date (at the time I'm writing this at least) no Congressman has even uttered the word "Bilderberg" on the floor of the House or the Senate, or anywhere publicly for that matter, other than Ron Paul and his son Rand as I previously mentioned.

President Dwight D. Eisenhower

President Dwight D. Eisenhower, best known for warning the world about the Military Industrial Complex in his 1961 farewell address, wrote a memo to his assistant in 1955 about that year's Bilderberg meeting which took place in Barbizon, France. While Eisenhower didn't mention them by name, it's pretty obvious who he was talking about in the memo when he says, "I understand next week Prince Bernhard is having a meeting at Barbizon, continuing his exploration looking toward improving European and American relations. If personally you can fit such a trip into

---

[44] John R. Rarick, *Congressional Record*, 92nd Congress, 1st Session, Wednesday, Volume 117, No. 133, 15 September 1971, pp. E9615-E9624

your schedule, I suggest you find the money and go to France."[45]

Even though he didn't mention "Bilderberg" by name, but he was clearly talking about them since Prince Bernhard was the founder and chairman of the Bilderberg Group at the time, and since the meeting was to focus on "European and American relations."

Just a friendly reminder, or a heads up if you're not aware—when leaving office in 1961 President Eisenhower warned, "In the councils of government, we must guard against the acquisition of unwarranted influence, whether sought or unsought, by the military–industrial complex. The potential for the disastrous rise of misplaced power exists, and will persist. We must never let the weight of this combination endanger our liberties or democratic processes. We should take nothing for granted. Only an alert and knowledgeable citizenry can compel the proper meshing of the huge industrial and military machinery of defense with our peaceful methods and goals so that security and liberty may prosper together."

Unfortunately this rings even more true today than it did over 50 years ago when he said it and with the lies and broken promises from both major

---

[45] Eisenhower memo from March 11th 1955

political parties in America regarding warrantless wiretapping, the use of drones to assassinate people (including American citizens) and the never ending and always expanding War on Terror sparked by the attacks on September 11th 2001, it is clear the military-industrial complex has grown exponentially in size and power since President Eisenhower warned about it back in 1961.

CALIFORNIA SENATOR BARBARA BOXER REFUSES TO ANSWER ANY QUESTIONS ABOUT BILDERBERG AND ESCAPES IN A "SENATORS ONLY" ELEVATOR IN THE HART SENATE BUILDING IN WASHINGTON D.C.

LUKE RUDKOWSKI'S LIVESTREAMING RIG HE USED TO BROADCAST THE 2012 BILDERBERG PROTEST TO VIEWERS ON THE INTERNET.

Actions and Effects

What's talked about at Bilderberg or the consensus that the group comes too, often soon finds its way into becoming policy around the world. From the decades of leaked documents and insider revelations it appears that the birth of new legislation, economic booms and busts, and even the start of new wars and military actions around the globe are often traced back to Bilderberg.

One of their primary goals has been to form a New World Order global government, and over the last sixty years they have made tremendous progress with most of their plans already accomplished. In today's information age with popular independent media outlets and social media keeping an eye on the Bilderberg Group, it's almost impossible now for them to stay a secret, but the decades of denials and media blackouts prove they have been deceptive from the start. Now that they are getting fairly well known, the denials and tactics of playing dumb have changed into trying to pass themselves off as an ordinary business conference like the G8, G20, or the Davos World Economic Forum.

51

David Rothkopf, the managing director of Kissinger and Associates, an international advising firm founded by the infamous Henry Kissinger, wrote a very interesting book in 2009 titled *Superclass: The Global Power Elite and the World They are Making,* where he discussed the ruling elite and the various organizations that largely influence the political and economic landscape of the world. While not revealing any earth shattering insider secrets, Rothkopf does confirm some of the persistent allegations made about the ruling class by so-called "conspiracy theorists."

He wrote, "A global elite has emerged over the past several decades that has vastly more power than any other group on the planet. Each of the members of the superclass has the ability to regularly influence the lives of millions of people in multiple countries worldwide. Each actively exercises this power, and they often amplify it through the development of relationships with others in this class."[46]

He continues, "That such a group exists is indisputable. Heads of state, CEOs of the world's largest companies, media barons, billionaires who are actively involved in their investments, technology, entrepreneur, oil potentates, hedge

---

[46] Rothkopf, David - *Superclass: The Global Power Elite and the World They are Making* Preface page xiv

fund managers, private equity investors, top military commanders, a select few religious leaders, a handful of renowned writers, scientists, and artists, even terrorist leaders and master criminals, meet the above criteria for membership."[47]

"In fact, [the Bilderberg Group, Trilateral Commission, and the World Economic Forum] are an important part of the story of the superclass. They are places to convene, places to network, places to cultivate relationships, places to share views. To paraphrase Mark Malloch Brown, they are the village greens of the global elite."[48]

"The reality of these meetings and what they reveal about the informal mechanisms of power is much more interesting than the hyped-up conspiracy theories and their hysterical visions of total control."[49]

---

[47] Rothkopf, David - *Superclass: The Global Power Elite and the World They are Making* Preface page xiv

[48] Rothkopf, David - *Superclass: The Global Power Elite and the World They are Making* Preface page 265

[49] Rothkopf, David - *Superclass: The Global Power Elite and the World They are Making* Preface page 265

He also admits that, "Bilderberg does its best to stay under the radar."[50]   While he denies that they are planning "world domination," he does say, "They share similar goals in many cases a similar view of the world and the direction it should take," and that "In linking together with one another, they aim not to conspire as a group but to enhance their own power by advantageous associations."[51]

Sociologist William Domhoff said that, "I believe there is a national upper class in the United States....this means that wealthy families from all over the country, and particularly from major cities like New York, San Francisco, Chicago, and Houston, are part of interlocking social circles which perceive each other as equals, belong to the same clubs, interact frequently, and freely intermarry."[52]

---

[50] Rothkopf, David - *Superclass: The Global Power Elite and the World They are Making* Preface page 277

[51] Rothkopf, David - *Superclass: The Global Power Elite and the World They are Making* Preface page 285-286

[52] Domhoff, William - *The Bohemian Grove and Other Retreats: A Study in Ruling-Class Cohesiveness* page 86

Domhoff writes that elite social clubs are informal centers of policy making,[53] and that these organizations are consensus-seeking and policy-planning organizations of the upper class.[54]

He concludes that, "I think it makes a very good case for the hypothesis that the social upper class is a ruling class, especially in light of the amazingly disproportionate amount of wealth and income controlled by that small group of families."[55]

Another sociologist named Peter Phillips from the University of California, Davis, who earned his Ph.D. by writing his doctoral dissertation on the Bilderberg Group's more informal sister organization, the Bohemian Grove, says, "Involvement of these socio-economic and political institutional leaders in the activities at the Grove [and Bilderberg] gives them extensive periods of off-the-record discussion time with campmates and other Bohemians [and Bilderbergers] about the prevailing social issues of the day... All of these chats and talks work toward

[53] Domhoff, William - *The Bohemian Grove and Other Retreats: A Study in Ruling-Class Cohesiveness* page 92

[54] Domhoff, William - *The Bohemian Grove and Other Retreats: A Study in Ruling-Class Cohesiveness* page 93

[55] Domhoff, William - *The Bohemian Grove and Other Retreats: A Study in Ruling-Class Cohesiveness* page 110

the building of a consensual mind set regarding current political and social issues....In other words the general parameters of major policy and socio-political decisions can and do evolve at the Bohemian Grove and [Bilderberg] Club."[56]

Phillips concludes that secret elite gatherings like the Bohemian Grove and the Bilderberg Group "are examples of how elite consensus building around key policy issues occur. After the weekend each participant could then return to his own power base and proceed with individual action rooted in consensual understandings obtained on the weekend."[57]

What kind of understandings is he talking about? Let's find out.

Creating a One World Government

Despite denials for decades that the economic and political elite were secretly working towards a global government, one of the founding members of the Bilderberg Group who sat on the steering

---

[56] Phillips, Peter - *A Relative Advantage: Sociology of the San Francisco Bohemian Club*. A Doctoral Dissertation (1994) Page 156-157

[57] Phillips, Peter - *A Relative Advantage: Sociology of the San Francisco Bohemian Club*. A Doctoral Dissertation (1994) Page 138

committee for 30 years once admitted that the critics aren't entirely wrong. In 2001 when talking to Jon Ronson, a documentary producer for the BBC and author of *Them: Adventures with Extremists*, Denis Healy said, "To say we were striving for a one-world government is exaggerated, but not wholly unfair. Those of us in Bilderberg felt we couldn't go on forever fighting one another for nothing and killing people and rendering millions homeless. So we felt that a single community throughout the world would be a good thing."[58]

An Establishment insider and mentor of President Bill Clinton named Carroll Quigley published a book in 1966 for fellow ruling class insiders titled *Tragedy & Hope: A History of the World in Our Time* in order to help them understand how the world works and the elite's vision for the future. Quigley, who was a professor at Georgetown University in Washington D.C. (the oldest Jesuit institution of higher learning in the United States—founded in 1789), knew that most of the general public doesn't read books or newspapers and are more interested in sports entertainment and celebrity news than what's happening in Washington D.C.

---

[58] *The Guardian* "Who Pulls the Strings?" by Jon Ronson (March 10th 2001)

Quigley alluded to the Bilderberg Group when he wrote, "There does exist, and has existed for a generation, an international Anglophile network which operates, to some extent, in the way the radical Right believes the Communists act. In fact, this network, which we may identify as the Round Table Groups, has no aversion to cooperating with the Communists, or any other groups, and frequently does so. I know of the operations of this network because I have studied it for twenty years and was permitted for two years, in the early 1960's, to examine its papers and secret records."

"I have no aversion to it or to most of its aims and have, for much of my life, been close to it and to many of its instruments. I have objected, both in the past and recently, to a few of its policies (notably to its belief that England was an Atlantic rather than a European Power and must be allied, or even federated, with the United States and must remain isolated from Europe), but in general my chief difference of opinion is that it wishes to remain unknown, and I believe its role in history is significant enough to be known."[59]

Regarding the Federal Reserve and the financial domination by a handful of international banks, he said, "The powers of financial

---

[59] Quigley, Carroll – *Tragedy and Hope* page 950

capitalism had a far-reaching aim, nothing less than to create a world system of financial control in private hands able to dominate the political system of each country and the economy of the world as a whole. This system was to be controlled in a feudalist fashion by the central banks of the world acting in concert, by secret agreements arrived at in frequent meetings and conferences. The apex of the systems was to be the Bank for International Settlements in Basel, Switzerland, a private bank owned and controlled by the world's central banks which were themselves private corporations. Each central bank...sought to dominate its government by its ability to control Treasury loans, to manipulate foreign exchanges, to influence the level of economic activity in the country, and to influence cooperative politicians by subsequent economic rewards in the business world."[60]

Quigley's *Tragedy & Hope* is not a book "exposing" a "conspiracy" but rather a history book for elitists to help them understand how the Establishment works and what their plans are.

---

[60] Quigley, Carroll – *Tragedy and Hope* page 324

European Union

Documents from the 1955 Bilderberg meeting discovered at the estate of a deceased member show they were planning the European Union and a central currency back in the 1950s, decades before the EU was formed and their new Euro currency introduced.[61] The documents came from the personal files of former Labour Party leader Hugh Gaitskell which had been stored at a local University after his death. They are marked "Personal and strictly confidential," and "Not for publication either in whole or in part," and were made available to the BBC during an investigation in 2003.[62] Wikileaks also obtained the documents and then published them through their website.[63]

Gaitskell was part of Bilderberg's steering committee and had attended the very first meeting in 1954 and kept years of the itineraries which

---

[61] PrisonPlanet.com "Leaked 1955 Bilderberg Docs Outline Plan For Single European Currency" by Paul Joseph Watson (May 8th 2009)

[62] BBC Radio 4 Investigation "Club Class" by Simon Cox (2003) Audio available here: http://www.propagandamatrix.com/bbc_radio_4_bilderberg.mp3

[63] https://wikileaks.org/wiki/Bilderberg_meeting_report_Garmisch-Patenkirchen,_1955

included his own handwritten notes about the different speakers and topics. Historian Dr. Hugh Wilford showed Simon Cox of BBC Radio 4 the archive. "This is from Hugh Gaitskell to his friend and Labour Party colleague Dennis Healey in which he's telling him about the conference. He describes it as a rather special kind of conference, very hand-picked with the proceedings private, and ends by saying that he hopes that he'll be able to give Healey further details but meanwhile would you please treat the whole matter as absolutely confidential—say nothing about it to anybody," explains Wilford.

Simon Cox: "So, real secrecy from the very beginning."

Hugh Wilford: "Yes."

Simon Cox: "Because you can see when you hear about the way that it's set up, why people have these conspiracy theories."

Hugh Wilford: "Yes, now I can quite see why that is the case, and the fact that so much secrecy was insisted upon for these early meetings, and I mean it doesn't really necessarily look very good that the leader of the British Labour Party is consorting with various representatives of the secret services and American Capitalists and doing so in such a clandestine fashion, so yes, I can see why conspiracy theorists have sprung up and surrounded Bilderberg."[64]

Simon Cox: "The papers show exactly what was discussed within the secret confines of Bilderberg. What's striking is the degree of consensus reached by those at the meeting on contentious topics like European integration... Here's another paper from the first ones about the European Union. It's interesting here saying some sort of European Union has long been a Utopian dream, but at the conference it was agreed it was now a necessity of our times. So this is 50 years ago saying we must have a European Union."

Hugh Wilford: "Yes, again reflecting the fact that many of the people involved in planning Bilderberg had also played leading roles in getting the European movement going in the late 1940s and early 50s."

Simon Cox, the BBC investigator, concluded, "Without Bilderbergers, Europe could be a very different place."

Two years after the documents discovered in Gaitskell's estate were drawn up for the 1955 meeting, the European Union started to take shape with the creation of the European Economic

------

[64] BBC Radio 4 "Club Class" with Simon Cox (2003) - Around 9 minute mark - http://www.propagandamatrix.com/bbc_radio_4_bilderberg.mp3

Community (EEC) in 1957 which merged the markets of six European countries—France, Germany, Italy, Belgium, the Netherlands and Luxembourg. This later grew into the European Union in 1993 containing 28 nation states: Austria, Belgium, Bulgaria, Croatia, Cyprus, Czech Republic, Denmark, Estonia, Finland, France, Germany, Greece, Hungary, Ireland, Italy, Latvia, Lithuania, Luxembourg, Malta, Netherlands, Poland, Portugal, Romania, Slovakia, Slovenia, Spain, Sweden, and the United Kingdom.

Sociologist Mike Peters from Leeds Beckett University in England confirms, "The single currency [the Euro] was rooted first by people who were connected with Bilderberg," and concludes, "The sheer wealth and importance of the people who attend Bilderberg suggest that this is one of the most important political forums in the modern world."[65]

Documents from Bilderberg's less secretive sister organization, the Council on Foreign Relations, reveal they have plans for several other massive regional unions around the world, including the Eastern European Union, the Middle Eastern Union, an Asian-Pacific Union, African

---

[65] BBC Radio 4 "Club Class" with Simon Cox (2003) - Around 9 minute mark - http://www.propagandamatrix.com/ bbc_radio_4_bilderberg.mp3 (at approximately the 11:15 mark)

Union, South American Union, and a North American Union. Part of this plan includes unifying the currencies of each of these different unions as well. For example, in the case of the North American Union—Canada, the United States and Mexico would all use what has been proposed as the amero for all financial transactions.[66]

The idea is, once these various regional unions are formed, and their currencies unified, the final step will be to merge the unions (along with each of their respective currencies) into one global governing body, and at the same time introduce a global currency in the form of a digital dollar, ushering in the era of a completely cashless society.[67] Some have proposed this new global currency be called the Phoenix, named after the mythological bird which is said to rise from the ashes of its predecessor after death in a cycle of rebirth and renewal.[68] From ashes of the death of

---

[66] Pastor, Robert - *Toward a North American Community: Lessons from the Old World for the New* page 115

[67] *New York Times* "Cashless Society? It's Already Coming" by Damon Darlin (November 28th 2014)

[68] *The Economist* - "Get Ready for the Phoenix" (January 9th 1988) Volume 306 pages 9-10)

all previous currencies, the new global currency will emerge.

Selecting World Leaders

Many consider Bilderberg to be the Kingmakers or the place where a consensus is made about which political candidate the Establishment will throw their support behind and which ones they'll throw under the bus. With the power to make major editorial decisions in the newsrooms of the world's primary media outlets and by controlling the purse strings of the big banks and political financiers, they "can make or break presidents, popes, or prime ministers," as the character Howard Beale famously warned in the classic 1976 film *Network*.

George Bush Senior attended in 1985 and became president in 1988. Bill Clinton attended in 1991 and then became president a year later. Tony Blair was invited in 1993 and became Prime Minister of England in 1997. Romano Prodi attended in 1999 and later that year he became president of the European Union Commission. In 2004, Senator John Edwards spoke with the group and was later chosen to be the Democratic vice presidential nominee by presidential candidate John Kerry, who—like his opponent George W.

Bush—is a member of the Skull & Bones society which made it a win/win for the Establishment no matter who was chosen to be president.[69]

There was a surprising little mention of John Edwards covert visit by a reporter for the *New York Times* in an article about the VP selection process which noted, "Several people pointed to the secretive and exclusive Bilderberg conference of some 120 people that this year drew the likes of Henry A. Kissinger, Melinda Gates and Richard A. Perle to Stresa, Italy, in early June, as helping win Mr. Kerry's heart. Mr. Edwards spoke so well in a debate on American politics with the Republican Ralph Reed that participants broke Bilderberg rules to clap before the end of the session. Beforehand, Mr. Edwards traveled to Brussels to meet with NATO officials, brandishing his foreign-policy credentials."[70]

The article then quoted an anonymous source and associate of John Kerry who was in attendance for Edwards' debate, who said, "His performance at Bilderberg was important," and

---

[69] *The Telegraph* "The secret society that ties Bush and Kerry" by Charles Laurence (February 1st 2004)

[70] *New York Times* "THE 2004 ELECTION: THE PROCESS; Aide in the Selection of a Running Mate Recalls, 'We Never Got to a Short List'" by Jodi Wilgoren (July 7th 2004)

admitted it was largely responsible for him being chosen as the candidate for Kerry's vice president.[71]

And, as mentioned earlier, it is also widely believed that Barack Obama attended in 2008 after he slipped away from the press for a secret meeting that neither he nor his spokesman would give any details about. Could it really be just a "coincidence" that his disappearance for this mysterious meeting was at the exact time Bilderberg was in session about a half hour away?

Jim Tucker reported that in 1989 one of the agendas on the menu was ousting British Prime Minister Margaret Thatcher because she opposed surrendering Britain's sovereignty to the European Union by refusing to join the EU.[72] The following year people within her own party conspired, and succeeded, to replace her with John Major, who then helped facilitate the rise of the European Union, fulfilling Bilderberg's long-held dream.

Again, Carroll Quigley openly revealed how it was to the elite's advantage to have only two political parties for people to choose from and how they would be engineered to intersect at their core. The reason being, he said was, "The two

---

[71] Ibid.

[72] Tucker, Jim - *Jim Tucker's Bilderberg Diary* page 57

parties should be almost identical, so that the American people can 'throw the rascals out' at any election without leading to any profound or extensive shifts in policy."[73]

The meeting, which moves from country to country around Europe and the United States, is usually held nearby Washington D.C. on election years, which certainly can't be a coincidence. Even if presidential candidates themselves don't go, they often send their representatives to lobby to Bilderberg and highlight their associate's usefulness and to report back to them after the meeting about what issues were discussed and what the consensus was on each topic.

The Iraq War

At the 2002 meeting, leaks revealed the consensus arrived was that the invasion of Iraq wouldn't happen until Spring of 2003 when many in the mainstream media were anticipating the war would start in the late summer or early Fall of 2002.[74]   Jim Tucker reported that Donald

---

[73] Quigley, Carroll – *Tragedy and Hope* pages 1247-1248

[74] The Iraq Resolution or the Iraq War Resolution (formally the Authorization for Use of Military Force Against Iraq Resolution of 2002) enacted October 16th 2002

Rumsfeld, who was then the Secretary of Defense, assured the Bilderberg Group that the invasion wouldn't happen until the following year,[75] which of course it did. Apparently some of the European allies needed more time to convince their people the invasion was "necessary" or to prepare to take advantage of the situation economically once it occurred.

As the world now knows, every reason given to justify the invasion of Iraq was a lie; from the hoaxes and fear mongering about their supposed weapons of mass destruction,[76] to the fabricated yellow cake uranium documents,[77] to the debunked claims about Saddam Hussein being involved with Al Qaeda and connected to the September 11th attacks.[78] Some people point to the little known Washington D.C. based Neocon think tank the Project for the New American Century (PNAC for short) as laying out the strategy years earlier to maintain America's

---

[75] Tucker, Jim - *Jim Tucker's Bilderberg Diary* page 9

[76] *CNN* "Report: No WMD stockpiles in Iraq" (October 7th 2007)

[77] *CNN* "Fake Iraq documents 'embarrassing' for U.S. by David Ensor (March 14th 2003)

[78] *Washington Post* "Bush Reasserts Hussein-Al Qaeda Link" by Walter Pincus and Dana Milbank (June 17th 2004)

dominance in the world by preemptively attacking foreign countries or inserting America's military "even in conflicts that otherwise do not directly engage U.S. interests."[79]

One PNAC document titled *Rebuilding America's Defenses* (written in September of 2000) seems to suggest they needed a major catastrophe to occur in order to justify carrying out their plans. At one point it says, "Furthermore, the process of transformation, even if it brings revolutionary change, is likely to be a long one, absent some catastrophic and catalyzing event— like a new Pearl Harbor."[80]

Of course, this "new Pearl Harbor" was the September 11th attack on the World Trade Center in New York City which has been cited as the reason for just about every restriction of liberty and expansion of military power ever since.[81] Many people believe the attacks were allowed to happen on purpose in order to provide a pretext

---

[79] *Washington Post* "Keeping the U.S. First; Pentagon Would Preclude a Rival Superpower" by Barton Gellman (March 11th 1992)

[80] *Rebuilding America's Defenses* by the Project for the New American Centuary page 51

[81] *Washington Post* "10 reasons the U.S. is no longer the land of the free" by Jonathan Turley (January 13th 2012)

(reason) for implementing the Project for the New American Century's plans, but this is whole other issue in and of itself.[82]

At the 2004 White House Correspondence dinner, the annual red carpet event where the White House wines and dines mainstream media reporters who are supposed to act as watch dogs carefully monitoring the government's actions, President George W. Bush was cracking jokes about not finding any WMDs in Iraq. When he was at the podium addressing the crowd, a photo of him bending over looking under his desk in the Oval Office was put up on the screen as he said, "Those weapons of mass destruction got to be somewhere." The audience laughs and applauds.[83]

"Nope. No weapons over there." The laugher continues. Then another photo is shown of him bending over in an awkward position in another part of his office. "Maybe over here," he says, as a devilish grin appears on his face. Much of the audience again laughs.

---

[82] *Seattle Post-Intelligencer* "New Poll: A Third of U.S. Public Believes 9/11 Conspiracy Theory" by Thomas Hargrove (August 2nd 2006)

[83] *USA Today* "Bush's joke about WMD draws criticism" (March 26th 2004)

THESE PROTESTERS THINK BILDERBERG ARE "SCUM."

ME TALKING TO THE POLICE GUARDING THE MEETING TO LET THEM KNOW WHO THEY ARE PROTECTING.

Talk Show Hosts Play Dumb

Radio talk shows provide an interesting platform for news and commentary, and the most-listened to shows have audiences of millions and often include popular politicians (and even presidents) as their guests. A popular feature of the show's format is that most of them take calls from the audience live on the air—well, live with a seven second delay, and calls that are pre-screened by a producer who first decides which ones will be put through to the host.

Many people are unaware that before a host puts a caller on the air, a producer first takes the call and if the question or comment is approved, that call is added to the call bank along with a note for the host about what the person wants to say. Occasionally myself and others have managed to get on the air with some of these hosts and instead of asking the question the producer approved during the screening process—we asked about Bilderberg or other blacklisted topics. Transcripts to some of those calls will follow, along with some footnotes which will show you where you can go to hear the archived audio clips for yourself.

Glenn Beck

When hosting his popular television show on the Fox News Channel, Glenn Beck once claimed that talking about the Bilderberg Group was going down a "tin foil hat road," and said he didn't care about the Bilderberg Group, and then compared them to a toy company.

In July 2010 he said, "The Bilderbergers had their meeting, I don't really know much about these people, and I don't really care. I know probably more about the Build a Bear people in the malls, and I know those people are brainwashing our kids with teddy bears. I don't know what kind of secret meetings they have to get our kids into the bear industry, but I don't like it. If the Bilderberg's are half as evil as the teddy bear people, look out."[84]

Beck then went on to say that those inside the Bilderberg meeting were probably talking about how to help the world. On his syndicated radio show he later joked that the Bilderberg Group were shapeshifting Reptilians.

---

[84] *Fox News Channel* "Glenn Beck Program" (June 2010)

Sean Hannity

On January 29th 2009 I got through on Sean Hannity's radio show and asked him very nicely if could explain what the Bilderberg Group is and what they do. The call can be heard on YouTube and here is a transcript:[85]

Hannity: Mark, KFMB San Diego, next on the Sean Hannity Show—how are you Mark?

Mark: Pretty good, but with all this economic crises going on and everyone looking for answers and blame, I was wondering if you could talk about the Bilderberg Group and the role that they play in the global economy and geopolitics?

Hannity: I have no idea what you're talking about. [drops call]. Let's go to Amy in Cincinnati on 55KRC, what's up Amy?

Michael Savage

After years of denying that Bilderberg had any significance or influence at all, Michael Savage

---

[85] YouTube: Sean Hannity: What Bilderberg Group (Call made January 29th 2009 and posted to YouTube on February 2nd 2009. https://youtu.be/WZiwwY_ajBI

later changed his tune and spoke quite candidly about them in 2010. A transcript of a call I made to him in 2009 went as follows:[86]

Savage: Right here on the Savage Nation—San Diego—Mark, go ahead please.

Mark: Let's talk about the Bilderberg Group. You're talking about conspiracies to bankrupt the economy—what can you tell the audience about the Bilderberg Group and why isn't that mentioned ever in any mainstream media?

Savage: Well that's like talking about the Council on Foreign Relations. It's too esoteric for the audience. I don't think we have to go any further than Obama, [Timothy] Geithner, Nancy Pelosi, Dianne Feinstein, and Hillary Clinton, is that enough for you? We don't need a Bilderberg Group, we have the Democrat socialist group that I just mentioned.

Mark: Every year the Bilderberg Group meets in secret and Obama has [gets cut off]

---

[86] YouTube: Michael Savage now admits Bilderberg Group is in control of the economy, the media, and White House. https://youtu.be/W5cTLlaRbAg

Savage: We know this. We understand it but I don't want to talk about some esoteric group called the Bilderberg Group. What good is going to come of talking about the Bilderberg Group which I've heard since 1990? Tell me what good's going to come of it?

Mark: Why don't we expose them? Maybe they're violating the Logan Act [cut off again]

Savage: What needs to be exposed is Obama's hypocrisy, so that the idiots finally get it and stop him before he does more damage. That's what needs to be done. Not talking about some esoteric conspiracy group! You're 100% wrong! Thanks for the call. [Savage drops the call]

Just one year later he had a totally different view. In a monologue in 2010 which was recorded and uploaded to YouTube by a listener, Savage said, "I gotta tell you, for the last few years I've been going through thoughts about leaving radio. I'm bored. Burned out. Sick of Obama. Sick of the communists and the Bilderberg Group taking over the media and the government. But something is happening. The Bilderberg schemers are losing control of the global game. The puppet masters are losing control of the marionettes. When you see that the

Bilderbergs are meeting secretly right now and many of the same people who brought about the economic collapse [of 2008] by rigging the system are there doing it again—the same people who put Obama in power are there again, you have to understand the danger you're in."[87]

Rush Limbaugh

In 2010 Rush Limbaugh (who signed a $400 million dollar contract with Clear Channel in 2008 to do another eight-years of radio)[88] gave a rather lengthy monolog about the Bilderberg Group after reading an article saying that Fidel Castro, the longtime Communist Cuban dictator, had just discovered them and expressed concerns about their power. Rush made Bilderberg sound like a big joke and something only "kooks" believed in, and appeared to attempt to link anyone who was interested or suspicious of the Bilderberg Group

---

[87] YouTube: Michael Savage admits Bilderberg put Obama in Power https://www.youtube.com/watch?v=kSYFZY5oTR0

[88] *The Wall Street Journal* "Clear Channel, Limbaugh Ink $400 Million New Contract" by Sarah McBride (July 3rd 2008)

with Fidel Castro. A partial transcript of his monologue follows:[89]

Rush: I saw this yesterday afternoon and last night. The headline intrigued me. I read it and I started laughing out loud. "Fidel Castro Fascinated by Book on Bilderberg Club." This is from the *Associated Press:* "Fidel Castro is showcasing a theory long popular both among the far left and far right: that the shadowy Bilderberg Group has become a kind of global government, controlling not only international politics and economics, but even culture. The 84-year-old former Cuban president published an article Wednesday that used three of the only eight pages in the Communist Party newspaper Granma to quote—largely verbatim—from a 2006 book by Lithuanian-born writer Daniel Estulin. Estulin's work, 'The Secrets of the Bilderberg Club,' argues that the international group largely runs the world. It has held a secretive annual forum of prominent politicians, thinkers and businessmen since it was founded in 1954 at the Bilderberg Hotel in Holland."[90]

---

[89] Rush Limbaugh Transcript from August 20th 2010 (Posted on RushLimgaugh.com http:// www.rushlimbaugh.com/daily/2010/08/20/ fidel_castro_discovers_bilderberg_conspiracy_to_popularize _beatles

[90] Rush Limbaugh Transcript from August 20th 2010

This gets better. (laughing)   They run the world, and they didn't tell Castro.   He's just learning it here at 84 and he finds it fascinating. "Castro offered no comment on the excerpts other than to describe Estulin as honest and well-informed and to call his book a 'fantastic story.' Estulin's book, as quoted by Castro, described 'sinister cliques and the Bilderberg lobbyists manipulating the public 'to install a world government that knows no borders and is not accountable to anyone but its own self.' The Bilderberg group's website says its members have 'nearly three days of informal and off-the-record discussion about topics of current concern' once a year, but the group does nothing else." So they get together three days a year and control the world (joking).

They had a conspiracy, they didn't tell Fidel about it, and he's only learning about it now when he's retired and can't join it and do anything about it. Walter Lippmann created the Beatles to distract people.   Not only that, the Bilderbergs created feminism to get men and women at war with one another to distract us while they destroyed world economies. That did work. (laughing)

Folks, from the very first day, back in Kansas City, when I uttered my first political comment on the radio, I was set upon by these conspiracy people. Oh-ho-ho-ho yes. They no longer bother with me. (Off air question by producer in Rush's ear) I've never been to a Bilderberg meeting, Snerdley. No. I've never been to the Socialists International. I've never been to a CFR meeting or Trilateralist Commission meeting. Remember, I'm the guy that came up with the kook test. Yeah, the kook test was to distract people from me being part of the conspiracy. Yeah. Remember one of the questions on the kook test? (laughing) If trilateralist A is driving west at 60 miles an hour and the Council on Foreign Relations member B is driving east at 40 miles an hour, how long does it take for both of them to take over the world?

Alan Colmes

I personally called the Alan Colmes radio show and got on the air several times to try to get him on record about the issue. Colmes once hosted a show with Sean Hannity on the Fox News Channel called *Hannity & Colmes* between 1996 and 2009 but he was dropped by the network and the show renamed just *Hannity.* One call made on February 2nd 2009, which I saved from the show's archive and posted on YouTube, goes as follows:[91]

Alan: Hello.

Mark: Don't the American people deserve to know that Obama met with the Bilderberg Group and why is it that you won't talk about them ever?

Alan: Because we talk about them when people like you call up to spread these crazy conspiracy theories. [Colmes drops the call]

Someone else once got on the air and asked him a very normal, rational question about Bilderberg. Someone (perhaps the caller himself) posted the audio on YouTube in 2012. Colmes again ridicules the caller:[92]

Caller: I was curious—what's your take on the theory that the Bilderberg Group basically groomed Obama [Colmes cuts off the caller]

---

[91] YouTube: Alan Colmes: Bilderberg Group a Conspiracy Theory
https://www.youtube.com/watch?v=kaBQ-Z1YsYM

[92] YouTube: Alan Colmes & The Bilderbergers (posed by bricksquad305 on June 23rd 2012) https://www.youtube.com/watch?v=JoQ3dMUFZ8A

Colmes: Oh, cut it out with the Bilderbergers already, it's a bunch of crap. C'mon.

Caller: Well you hear a lot about it.

Alan: Yeah, yeah, you hear a lot about it from conspiracy freaks.

Dennis Miller

A caller in 2009 got on the air on the Dennis Miller show and asked him about Bilderberg as well. Here is a transcript of that call, which can also be heard on YouTube.[93]

Miller: Keith in Texas, what's up?

Caller: Hey Dennis. Great show. I went to my first Tea Party July 4th and I learned a lot of things, but I came out worried because as a Texan, here we have Rick Perry and he's running for governor against Kay Bailey Hutchisun, and some people say he's going to be running for president possibly. The thing that bothers me is I saw on News 8 in Austin—local news here—about him

---

[93] YouTube: Dennis Miller show crashed by Bilderberg truth (posted August 11th 2009) https://www.youtube.com/watch?v=eekTMXzMM00

attending the Bilderberg conference, and that concerns me because [Miller cuts off caller and drops the call].

Miller: Aw, that's creeping me out, I'm sorry baby, I'm going to rock. I need my "burgs" with an "erg" at the end, as in James Cameron's *Titanic*. Once you start spelling it otherwise I get conspiracy and I don't have time right now. You know there's certain words as soon as you hear them. When a guy says "Bilderbergian" and you say 'can you explain that' and they keep going, you know that they...in the middle of appearing measured, he's dropped a huge steaming ideological cow pie, and you should move on from it. Alright. Dennis Miller Show. [Cuts to commercial]

Fareed Zarkaria

Just before the 2011 Bilderberg meeting, CNN's Fareed Zakaria wrote a blog on CNN.com titled "Why do we embrace conspiracy theories?" which started out saying how a lot of people on Facebook and Twitter were asking him about President Obama's birth certificate being faked and saying they thought Osama Bin Laden's death was possibly staged.

"The propensity of Americans to embrace conspiracy theories has long been attributed to their great suspicion of state authority," he says. "America was founded as a revolt against centralized power and there has always been a fear of coordinated action taking place in the dark behind closed doors. American conspiracy theories implicate Wall Street, the Federal Reserve, the U.S. government, the intelligence community and many others."[94]

He continues, "I can't tell you how many times people ask me about the conspiracy of the Bilderberg Group. It is a conference I've occasionally been invited to and have attended once or twice." He admits he has attended once or twice? You'd think a person would remember if they've been to the historic Bilderberg meeting once or if they came back a second time since it's kind of a big deal.

He went on to say, "If only the people who wrote the alarmist treatises on the Bilderberg Group were allowed in. They would be so utterly disappointed. It's just a conference like dozens of others around the world. And anyway, the idea that a finance minister or a banker would say something with a group of 150 people that is any

---

[94] CNN.com "Why do we embrace conspiracy theories?" by Fareed Zakaria (May 6th 2011)

different than what he would say in public is crazy in today's world where everything leaks instantly. In my experience, they say the same fairly banal platitudes inside as they say outside."[95]

Fareed says that inside the meeting men speak the same way they do in public? And they don't say anything at Bilderberg they don't say publicly? Why the Chatham House Rule then? Why all the secrecy and denials for decades? Why not just broadcast Bilderberg live on C-SPAN if it's "just another conference" like dozens of others around the world?

He concludes his blog post saying, "So on the few occasions in my life when I've been inside centers of the conspiracy, I've been disappointed and relieved to find they were pretty much like the world on the outside."[96]

---

[95] Ibid.

[96] Ibid.

Bilderberg's Goals

A Global Socialist Government

Often called the "New World Order," a primary goal of the Bilderberg elite is to integrate all the world's governments into one unified system. The United Nations was basically the beginning of this, but in order to accomplish the final phase of their plan, the sovereignty of the United States and all other countries would have to be eliminated—and their laws, militaries, and Constitutions all placed under a single planetary political authority.

The New World Order plan also consists of making this super State a socialist system that will function as a Nanny State which will "take care" of all humanity through massive redistribution of wealth, huge subsidies, and unlimited free handouts to those who don't work, funded through exorbitant taxes on those who do.

Presidents from George Bush Senior to Bill Clinton and Barack Obama have all publicly proclaimed that their goal is to form a New World

Order, and the justification is always a current crisis that this New Age will supposedly solve. Just three days after the 9/11 attacks in 2001, the co-chair of the Council on Foreign Relations (and Bilderberg member) Gary Hart stated, "There is a chance for the President of the United States to use this disaster—to carry out what his father—a phrase his father used I think only once, and it hasn't been used since—and that is a New World Order."[97]

Longtime Bilderberg member and financier Henry Kissinger stated that the problems Barack Obama's administration was facing regarding the ongoing War on Terror and the economic collapse of 2008, "can give new impetus to American foreign policy partly because the reception of him is so extraordinary around the world. His task will be to develop an overall strategy for America in this period when, really, a New World Order can be created. It's a great opportunity, it isn't just a crisis."[98]

This is the same man who, according to Bob Woodward and Carl Bernstein—the reporters who blew open the Watergate scandal, refers to

---

[97] *CSPAN*: Gart Hart calls for the use of 9/11 to carry out a New World Order (Available on YouTube) https://www.youtube.com/watch?v=5r7htckec-U

[98] CNBC in February 2009 - video on YouTube.

members of the U.S. military as "dumb, stupid animals" who are used as pawns for America's foreign policy.[99]

Perhaps the most infamous admission is when George Bush Senior stated the purpose of the Gulf War was to implement the "big idea" of the "New World Order." James Warburg, the son of Paul Warburg, the "father" of the Federal Reserve Bank, said at an appearance before the U.S. Senate Committee on Foreign Relations that, "We shall have world government, whether or not we like it. The question is only whether world government will be achieved by consent or by conquest."[100]

One of the problems is that in order for this to happen, some of the freedoms and policies we cherish in the United States will have to be eliminated and repealed. During his acceptance speech when receiving the United Nations Global Governance Award in 1999, the former anchor for CBS News—Walter Cronkite—told the audience that all the countries in the world, "are going to

[99] Bob Woodward & Carl Bernstein - *The Final Days* second Touchstone paperback edition (1994) Chapter 14, pp. 194-195

[100] Senate Report (Senate Foreign Relations Committee) (February 17th 1950). Revision of the United Nations Charter: Hearings Before a Subcommittee of the Committee on Foreign Relations, Eighty-First Congress. United States Government Printing Office. p. 494.

have to be convinced to give up some of that sovereignty to the better, greater union, and it's not going to be easy."[101]

We've already seen the United Nations try to change laws in the United States claiming their authority exceeds that of our state and federal governments. For example, after Colorado, Washington, Oregon, and Alaska legalized recreational marijuana use, the UN declared it was against international law and is trying to assert their authority over the states' decision to legalize pot.[102]

The UN continues to adopt new "hate speech laws" which seek to criminalize speech (and books) that some see as "discriminatory," which is an obvious violation of America's First Amendment, but in the age of political correctness gone amuck, many in the United States and other supposedly "free" countries are actually supporting such tyrannical legislation.[103]

---

[101] Norman Cousins Global Governance Award in 1999

[102] *Reuters* "U.S. states' pot legalization not in line with international law: U.N. agency" (November 12th 2014)

[103] *National Post* "Supreme Court upholds Canada's hate speech laws in case involving anti-gay crusader" by Joseph Brean (February 27th 2013)

It must be emphasized that this "global government" is not something that started at the grass roots level and has worked its way up the channels of government—it is exactly the opposite. The plan was started (in secret) at the very highest levels of powerful corporations and private organizations which function to influence international policy for their own benefit.

The plan for a New World Order global government is also something that was called "just a conspiracy theory" for decades, but in recent years it is now obviously happening and being promoted by countless politicians and heads of international corporations as something the average citizen should embrace with open arms.

Global Currency and Cashless Society

As previously mentioned, the personal papers of UK's Labour Party leader Hugh Gaitskell revealed that ever since their beginning in the 1950s, Bilderberg was working towards the creation of a unified Europe and common currency.[104] In more recent years they have been tirelessly attempting to replicate that formula with

---

[104] BBC Radio 4 "Club Class" with Simon Cox (2003) - Around 9 minute mark - http://www.propagandamatrix.com/ bbc_radio_4_bilderberg.mp3

other regional territories and currencies, with the ultimate goal of finally merging them all into one global digital currency and eliminating cash and coins (as well as gold and silver) as mediums of exchange. On the surface, a global unified currency may seem appealing due to its ability to be used universally anywhere throughout the world without having to exchange currencies when traveling or spending money in different parts of the world, but there are many downsides which are often overlooked, ignored, or covered up.[105]

Credit and debit cards of course were the first phase of the cashless society, and recently a major leap occurred when Apple Pay and the Apple Watch rolled out in April of 2015.[106] Fewer and fewer people are using cash, or even carrying any of it in their wallet at all. A study in 2014 showed that almost half of Americans carry $20 or less on them when they leave the house, eighty percent carry less than $50, and about ten percent of

---

[105] *CNBC* "Cashless society: A huge threat to our freedom" by Scott A. Shay (December 12th 2013)

[106] *The Guardian* "Mobile payments: the brave new cashless future" by Christer Holloman (March 3rd 2015)

people carry no cash at all.[107]   Many Millennials and those in Generation Z see cash as old fashioned and something that grandma and grandpa used to buy things with before the digital age.

A growing number of banking officials are pushing hard to have cash eliminated as soon as possible.   In April of 2015 a top Citibank economist suggested that cash should be abolished, and in order to coerce people into going digital, he also proposed the use of cash should be taxed at such a high rate that it would discourage most people from using it at all.[108]   Jim Leaviss, a banker with M&G investments in the UK, soon followed by suggesting outright banning cash. "Forcing everyone to spend only by electronic means from an account held at a government-run bank would give the authorities far better tools to deal with recessions and economic booms," he said.[109]

---

[107] *Washington Post* "What's in your wallet? Probably not cash" by Jonnelle Marte (May 12th 2014)

[108] *Bloomberg* "Citi Economist Says It Might Be Time to Abolish Cash" by Lorcan Roche Kelly (April 10th 2015)

[109] *The Telegraph* "How to end boom and bust: make cash illegal" by Jim Leaviss (May 13th 2015)

He also suggested negative interest rates (i.e. fees) on anyone who kept large amounts of money in their checking or savings account, and proposed the government could fluctuate these fees in order to encourage people to spend the money they have, rather than just lose it on fees, if the government wanted people to pour more money into the economy. "And once all money exists only in bank accounts—monitored, or even directly controlled by the government—the authorities will be able to encourage us to spend more when the economy slows, or spend less when it is overheating," Leaviss concluded.[110]

For years now, when you're on an airplane, if you want to buy something from the snack cart, many of the flight attendants only accept debit or credit cards.[111] Many will literally not accept cash for the food or drinks. Buying anything with cash these days is seen as suspicious. Storing cash in safe deposit boxes is against the rules at many banks, and the FDIC even suggests against it and urges people to deposit any and all cash they may have into a bank account instead.

---

[110] Ibid.

[111] *Airline Reporter* "More and More Airlines Become Cashless" by David Parker Brown (May 28th 2009)

In fact there are countless cases of police confiscating people's cash when they haven't even been arrested or charged with a crime.[112] It's called Civil Asset Forfeiture, which allows police and other government agencies to literally confiscate the cash a person is carrying when they are pulled over for a routine traffic stop because the cash itself is seen as suspicious. Even if there is no evidence it was obtained by criminal means, police still have the authority to take it on the spot because the money itself is seen as evidence of a crime, even if no arrest is made and there is no actual evidence of a crime, and no one has claimed the person has committed one.[113]

If you just sold an old car, motorcycle, or boat for a few thousand dollars cash, or if you happen to be traveling with an envelope of it on your way to poker night with guys—if it is discovered by police during a routine traffic stop, they can (and do all the time) confiscate it, even if there are no illegal drugs, weapons, or any evidence at all that

---

[112] *The Washington Post* "Highway seizure in Iowa fuels debate about asset-forfeiture laws" by Robert O'Harrow Jr (November 10th 2014)

[113] *CNBC* "Police cash confiscations still on the rise" by Mark Fahey (May 19th 2015)

the money was obtained illegally.[114]   You are guilty until proven innocent.

In the past, concerns about the approaching cashless society were ridiculed when so-called "conspiracy theorists" in the 1990s and early 2000s would warn about it getting close, but now that it is actually being implemented, those decades of denials are ignored and the new system is being promoted from the top down as the key to a consumerist Utopia.

Did you just buy a pregnancy test?   Some medication to treat an embarrassing medical condition?   Are you seeing a psychiatrist or a therapist for some mental health issues or personal problems? Did you purchase some personal items for you and your spouse to use in the bedroom? Are you buying certain books that the government may misinterpret as suspicious?   In a cashless society, all of these transactions and more are basically made available—not only to the government—but to countless third parties such as advertisers and international corporations who have access to your entire purchasing history due

---

[114] *Chicago Tribune* "Highway robbery? Texas police seize black motorists' cash, cars" by Howard Witt (March 10th 2009)

to the terms of service you implicitly agreed to with the use of a debit or credit card.[115]

Not to mention, the centralization of all points of purchase and relying on one single digital network to facilitate them all is begging for trouble in the event there is a systemwide failure. A power outage, computer glitch, or a cyber-attack would be absolutely devastating to perhaps tens or hundreds of millions of people, completely crippling their ability to purchase gas or food, or even buy a bus ticket or subway pass to get home from school or work.

Global Military Force

In attempts to supposedly put an end to war, the plan is to unite all the different militaries around the world into one supranational security force that will be directed based on the decisions of the globalist leaders. The beginning of the "Global Police" can be seen with NATO soldiers and UN "Peacekeeper" troops which are

---

[115] *Consumerist* "Credit Cards To Sell Your Buying History So Online Advertisers Can Target You More Precisely" by Ben Popken (October 25th 2011)

comprised of people from many nations and may be deployed by any nation-state that is a partner.[116]

Agencies like DARPA (the Defense Advanced Research Projects Agency) are working to make these military men and women virtually invincible. The quest for Super Soldiers has led to the design of exoskeleton suits that give the people wearing them super strength and speed.[117] President Obama once joked that "We're building Ironman," referring to the Marvel comic book character who uses an exoskeleton suit to fight crime, but these systems are no longer science fiction.[118] It has also been proposed that military soldiers have neural interface implants wired into their brains, turning them into literal cyborgs by merging man with machine in a "Transhumanist upgrade."[119]

Department of Defense documents drawn up in 1996 detail their plans to implant neural

---

[116] NATO Response Force/Very High Readiness Joint Task Force: Fact Sheet http://aco.nato.int/page349011837.aspx

[117] *CNN* "Robot exoskeleton suits that could make us superhuman" by Matthew Ponsford (May 22nd 2013)

[118] *CNET* "HAL-5: The exoskeleton robot 'to suit you'" by Elizabeth Armstrong Moore (March 15th 2011)

[119] *Time* "2045: The Year Man Becomes Immortal" by Lev Grossman (February 10th 2011)

interfaces in soldiers' brains—and in the heads of the civilian population as well. One document titled *Information Operations: A New War-Fighting Capability* outlines technology they hoped to have in place by the year 2025, and reads, "The implanted microscopic brain chip performs two functions. First, it links the individual to the IIC [Information Integration Center] creating a seamless interface between the user and the information resources. In essence, the chip relays the processed information from the IIC to the user, second the chip creates a computer generated mental visualization based upon the user's request."[120]

The documents claim such things would help increase security, saying, "An implanted microscopic chip does not require security measures to verify whether the right person is connected to the IIC [Information Integration Center], whereas a room, helmet, or sunglasses requires additional time-consuming access control mechanisms to verify an individual's identity and level of control within the Cyber Situation."[121]

---

[120] *Information Operations: A New War-Fighting Capability* (Volume 3 of Air Force 2025) page 35

[121] *Information Operations: A New War-Fighting Capability* (Volume 3 of Air Force 2025) page 35

The document addressed the expected resistance to such devices, saying, "Implanting 'things' in people raises ethical and public relations issues. While these concerns may be founded on today's thinking, in 2025 they may not be as alarming," and goes on to say, "The civilian populace will likely accept any implanted microscopic chips that allow military members to defend vital national interests."[122]

The finale phase of the plan is to replace most human soldiers with Terminator-style artificially intelligent robots. This was thought to be science fiction just a few years ago, but has recently become a serious endeavor by the United States and militaries around the world.[123] Robotic soldiers, whether in the form of Unmanned Aerial Vehicles, TALON tank-like robots, or android Terminators, would follow orders without question, no matter how unethical or inhumane they were.[124]

---

[122] *Information Operations: A New War-Fighting Capability* (Volume 3 of Air Force 2025) page 38

[123] *Washington Times* "Gearing up for robot wars" by Bill Gertz (April 8th 2015)

[124] *Computer World* "AI Researcher Says Amoral Robots Pose a Danger to Humanity" by Sharon Gaudin (March 7th 2014)

Elon Musk, founder and CEO of Tesla Motors and SpaceX, revealed in his authorized biography that he is concerned that Google's planned artificially intelligent robot army may end up exterminating the human race if it gets out of control or perceives our species as a threat to its existence. "Please note that I am normally super pro technology and have never raised this issue until recent months. This is not a case of crying wolf about something I don't understand."[125] He equated creating artificial intelligence with "summoning a demon."[126]

Other leaders working in information technology and science have also recently expressed concerns that the creation of an AI could be disastrous for humans. Stephen Hawking has warned it could be the biggest mistake in the history of humanity,[127] Microsoft founder Bill Gates has stated he's not sure why more people

---

[125] *Mashable* "Elon Musk's secret fear: Artificial Intelligence will turn deadly in 5 years" by Adario Strange (November 11th 2014)

[126] *Cnet* "Elon Musk: 'We are summoning the demon' with artificial intelligence" by Eric Mack (October 26th 2014)

[127] *BBC* "Stephen Hawking warns artificial intelligence could end mankind" by Rory Cellan-Jones (December 2nd 2014)

aren't concerned,[128] and Apple cofounder Steve Wozniak, who once dismissed such fears as unfounded, has recently changed his mind due to the rapid advance of AI and is now warning an artificial intelligent entity could enslave the human race and treat us like pets.[129]

Elimination of Right to Bear Arms

In the New World Order "socialist Utopia" everyone will supposedly live in peace and harmony, with the global government taking care of everyone's needs and protecting them like a loving parent or big brother. A primary promise of this new era is that supposedly "nobody needs to own guns" except the government, which is said to be the only group that can be trusted to use them responsibly. In order to finally eliminate crime, officials claim they need to ban citizens from owning guns and repeal the Second Amendment in the name of peace and prosperity.

---

[128] *Washington Post* "Bill Gates on dangers of artificial intelligence: 'I don't understand why some people are not concerned'" by Peter Holley (January 29th 2015)

[129] *Washington Post* "Apple co-founder on artificial intelligence: 'The future is scary and very bad for people'" by Peter Holley (March 24th 2015)

Incrementally the Second Amendment of the Constitution has been slowly eroded, and with every gun tragedy that's turned into a national story, more and more restrictions are placed on gun owners and the types of guns and accessories that can be sold to the public.[130]   Instead of addressing the underlying causes of violence, the guns themselves are blamed and said to be the problem, not a symptom of it.

Many have tried to argue that the Second Amendment of the American Constitution does not declare that citizens have the right to own guns.[131]   This argument is absolutely absurd but continues to be repeated by those on the left who believe it was put in place to authorize *the government* to own guns, which is 100% the opposite of its purpose.[132]   It was specifically included in the Bill of Rights to ensure ordinary citizens have the right to own guns as a way to—

---

[130] *Fox News* "Gun makers facing new limits urged to relocate" (March 31st 2013)

[131] YouTube: Cass Sunstein: "The Second Amendment: The Constitution's Most Mysterious Right" Speech at University of Chicago Law School (Posted June 20th 2013)

[132] *Washington Post* "Supreme Court affirms fundamental right to bear arms" by Robert Barnes and Dan Eggen (June 29th 2010)

not only protect themselves and their families from burglars and thugs—but also to serve as a deterrent to prevent the federal, state, or local government from abusing its power and violating basic civil liberties of Americans.

Rapper Ice-T summed up the purpose of the Second Amendment during an interview on British television when he was asked by Krishnan Guru-Murthy, anchor of Channel 4 News, if he has any guns at home. "Yeah, it's legal in the United States. It's part of our Constitution. You know, the right to bear arms is because that's the last form of defense against tyranny. Not to hunt. It's to protect yourself from the police."[133]

In 1997 Britain basically outlawed all guns and the law has been a blueprint Bilderberg hopes to duplicate around the rest of the world.[134] Slowly but surely they are making progress with many political pundits on television repeating their talking points about how now is the time to follow

---

[133] *Mediaite* "Rapper Ice-T Defends Gun Rights After Colorado Shooting: 'The Last Form Of Defense Against Tyranny'" by Andrew Kirell (July 23rd 2012)

[134] *Boston Globe* "UK gun control offers model for US" by Anthony Faiola (February 17th 2013)

Britain's lead and round up Americans' guns for everyone's safety.[135]

Former Attorney General Eric Holder once stated on C-SPAN2 that the government needed a new strategy to change the way people thought about the Second Amendment, and concluded, "We have to be repetitive about this. We need to do this every day of the week, and just really brainwash people into thinking about guns in a vastly different way."[136]

CNN's Fareed Zakaria, who is a member of the Bilderberg Group,[137] the Council on Foreign Relations, and Skull & Bones' sister society Scroll & Key at Yale University, argues that the Bill of Rights are outdated and should be "fixed" in order to remove the Second Amendment to "modernize the Constitution for the 21st Century."[138]

---

[135] *NewsBusters.org* "Piers Morgan Admits He Wants UK-Style Gun Ban in the States" by Matt Hado (May 3rd 2013)

[136] *The Daily Caller* "Holder in 1995: 'Really brainwash people' to be anti-gun" by Matthew Boyle (March 18th 2012)

[137] *Politico* "The Bilderberg Group's media men" by Dylan Byers (May 21st 2012)

[138] *CNN* "Fareed Zakaria GPS: Is it Time To Correct the Constitution?" (June 20th 2011)

China's official government-run news agency, Xinhua, has also demanded the United States tighten up gun control laws in America.[139] The United Nations has long wanted the American Second Amendment repealed, and is attempting to do so incrementally through small arms treaties.[140] Before you say "this couldn't happen in America," stop and think about all the freedoms that have been lost over the last generation, and see how quickly people forget.

Population Reduction and Stabilization

Because of healthcare advances and the continued exponential expansion of the world's population, many Bilderbergers fear that the earth does not have the natural resources to sustain the current population, let alone if it continues to increase. As far back as the 1970s environmentalists and the political elite were warning the planet's population would soon

---

[139] *Xinhua* "Innocent blood demands no delay for U.S. gun control" (December 12th 2015)

[140] *Forbes* "U.N. Agreement Should Have All Gun Owners Up In Arms" by Larry Bell (June 7th 2011)

balloon out of control and cause a global catastrophe.[141]

The billionaire founder of CNN, Ted Turner (who has five children himself), once remarked, "There's too many people. That's why we have global warming. We have global warming because too many people are using too much stuff, if there were less people, they'd be using less stuff." After drastically cutting greenhouse gas emissions, he said "We've got to stabilize the population."[142]

He went on that, "Not doing it will be catastrophic. We'll be 8 degrees hotter in 10, not 10 but 30 or 40 years and basically none of the crops will grow. Most of the people will have died and the rest of us will be cannibals. Civilization will have broken down. The few people that are left will be living in a failed state like Somalia or Sudan. And living conditions will be intolerable. The droughts will be so bad there

---

[141] *Business Insider* "PROFESSOR: The World Is Overpopulated By 5 Billion People" by Sanya Khetani (April 27th 2012)

[142] *PBS* - Charlie Rose - Interview with Ted Turner (April 1st 2008)

will be no more corn growing. Not doing it will be like suicide."[143]

Agenda 21 is a program launched by the United Nations in 1992 to deal with what they call "sustainable development" around the world, focusing on changing consumption patterns, preserving natural resources, and moving to more renewable energy sources. Part of Agenda 21 (the 21 meaning the 21st century) includes implementing birth control programs to slow down the population growth. The United Nations Population Fund, which was supposed to provide supplies and services for reproductive health and birth control in third world countries, was discovered to have also been involved with secret sterilizations and forced abortions.[144]

President Obama's chief science advisor John Holdren once wrote a book which proposed adding sterilants to nations' water supplies,[145] forcing women to get sterilized after their second

---

[143] Ibid.

[144] *Population Research Institute* "Abortion Pushing UN Population Fund has Record Number of Donors" by Terry Vanderheyden (January 13th 2006)

[145] Holdren, John – *Ecoscience* page 787-788

child,[146] and making them have abortions if they got pregnant for a third time.[147] The book, titled *Ecoscience,* reads, "Indeed, it has been concluded that compulsory population-control laws, even including laws requiring compulsory abortion, could be sustained under the existing Constitution if the population crisis became sufficiently severe to endanger the society."[148] [Compulsory means forced or mandatory, by the way]

Some see even more sinister methods on the table in order to accomplish this goal. The mysterious Georgia Guidestones monument calls for a global population of only 500 million people. The strange monument consists of four giant slabs of granite which stand 19-feet-tall, laid out in a paddlewheel formation, each with 10 different commandments carved into each of their eight faces, each one in a different langue (English, Spanish, Chinese, Russian, Swahili, Hindi, Hebrew, and Arabic). The structure, sometimes called "America's Stonehenge," is also said to contain the "Guides to the New Age." It was built in 1980 and stands in the middle of nowhere in a

---

[146] Holdren, John – *Ecoscience* page 786-787

[147] Holdren, John – *Ecoscience* page 837

[148] Holdren, John – *Ecoscience* page 837

field in the state of Georgia and is the creation of an unknown man who said he represented an unnamed group who wanted the monument built. Some call it the 10 Commandments of the New World Order since some of the "Guides" call for a global government, a one world universal language, and says the overpopulation of humanity is a "cancer on the earth."

Total Surveillance Society

There will be no more privacy if Bilderberg gets their way; no more anonymity, no more secrets—at least for the majority of us "regular folk." Members of the Party [the government] in George Orwell's *Nineteen Eighty-Four* could actually turn off the Telescreens in their homes, a luxury ordinary citizens didn't have; and the billionaires of Bilderberg will likely include some safeguards to ensure their own privacy remains in place while the rest of the world is forced to live in a fish bowl with everything we say, everywhere we go, everything we do, and everything we buy recorded, catalogued, and stored indefinitely.[149]

-----

[149] *Wired* "The NSA Is Building the Country's Biggest Spy Center" by James Bamford (March 15 2012)

Facial recognition systems have been beta tested since the 1990s and are now fully operational and being used at Las Vegas casinos,[150] hotels,[151] shopping malls,[152] sporting events,[153] airports,[154] government buildings,[155] and on the streets of major cities.[156] Edward Snowden, the NSA whistle blower, confirmed what many had suspected for some time—the U.S. government had a science fiction-like system capable of recording all electronic communications and hacking into people's email, social media accounts, and cell phones with the

---

[150] *CBS News* "Smile! You're On Casino Camera" (February 26th 2001)

[151] *TechDirt* "Hotels Get Facial-Recognition Sales Pitch" by Carlo Longino (February 19th 2009)

[152] *Time* "Face Recognition Technology Comes to Malls and Nightclubs" by Jerry Brito (December 12th 2001)

[153] *ABC News* "Biometrics Used to Detect Criminals at Super Bowl" by Vickie Chachere (February 13th 2002)

[154] *Guardian* "Trapwire surveillance system exposed in document leak" by Charlies Arthur (August 13th 2012)

[155] Ibid

[156] Ibid

click of a few keys, and with virtually no oversight or constraints.[157]

Smart TVs and artificial intelligent personal assistants like Siri, Amazon Echo, and Jibo have the capability to remotely record the most personal of moments and conversations within people's homes and bedrooms.[158] Orwell's *Nineteen Eighty-Four*, which was published back in 1949, reads, "The telescreen received and transmitted simultaneously. Any sound that Winston made, above the level of a very low whisper, would be picked up by it, moreover, so long as he remained within the field of vision which the metal plaque commanded, he could be seen as well as heard... You had to live—did live, from habit that became instinct—in the assumption that every sound you made was overheard, and, except in darkness, every movement scrutinized."[159]

Of course the argument is always, "if you don't have anything to hide, then you have nothing to fear," but as Thomas Jefferson once stated—if

---

[157] *TechDirt* "NSA Whistleblower Ed Snowden: From My Desk I Could Wiretap Anyone: You, A Federal Judge Or The President Of The US" by Mike Masnick (June 10th 2013)

[158] *ABC News* "Dozens of Arrests in 'Blackshades' Hacking Around the World" by Aaron Katersky (May 19th 2014)

[159] Orwell, George - *Nineteen Eighty-Four* page 2

you give up liberty in the name of security, you will have neither. In the name of "safety" and convenience, most people have willingly given up every last bit of privacy in our digital age. Most haven't even considered what could happen if civil liberties continue to slip or if the government were to grow too powerful and get out of control.

The ability of government agencies to profile, Orwellianly discriminate against, or target individuals for IRS audits, ordinance violations, or other forms of harassment based on their religious, personal, or political views is a reality everyone is now vulnerable to getting swept up in.[160]

Most major software developers and hardware manufactures have been coerced into building backdoors into their products so the government can easily remotely access people's devices and cloud accounts, as well as bypass any encryption that has been applied to their files.[161] The NSA even has a program where they intercept laptop computers and other products customers order online and then install special spyware and

---

[160] *The Washington Post* "IRS admits targeting conservatives for tax scrutiny in 2012 election" by Zachary A. Goldfarb and Karen Tumulty (May 10th 2013)

[161] *TechCrunch* "NSA Subverts Most Encryption, Works With Tech Organizations For Back-Door Access, Report Says" by Gregory Ferenstein (September 5th 2013)

hardware on them and then package the items back up and send them on their way.[162]

William Binney, a former high-level NSA official who worked for the agency for more than 30 years, resigned in 2001 after he discovered the surveillance systems they were using gave the government the potential for what he called "a turnkey totalitarian state."[163] His home was raided by the FBI in 2007 after he was suspected of leaking classified information to the New York Times about the NSA's spying programs. He was never charged with a crime and the read was seen as a show of force to intimidate any potential whistleblowers from reviling what the NSA was doing.

Some even see the omnipresent surveillance system growing far beyond just eyes and ears, into something so strange it sounds like science fiction. Tech titans are working to give birth to an artificial intelligent "God" that they hope will solve humanity's problems and intimately watch over

---

[162] *Forbes* "NSA Intercepting Laptops Ordered Online, Installing Spyware" by Erik Kain (December 29th 2013)

[163] *Breitbart* "The Turnkey Totalitarian State" by John Sexton (June 6th 2013)

everyone like a guardian angel, using its super intelligence to do "what's best" for humanity.[164]

See my previous book *Big Brother: The Orwellian Nightmare Come True* if you would like to read the details of the shocking parallels between George Orwell's classic novel *Nineteen Eighty-Four* and our current society in terms of actual NSA high-tech spy systems, mind-reading machines, secret government projects, advanced weapons, and emerging artificial intelligence systems.

Mainstream Media Uniformity

To manage the minds of billions of people, the information those people receive about the world must be carefully managed. Information is power, and mass communication systems are central sources of this power. People often point to Communist countries and their state-run media as examples of propaganda, while thinking places like the United States has a "free press," but the fact is the mainstream media in America is carefully controlled as well.

---

[164] *The Guardian* "AI scientists want to make gods. Should that worry us?" by Wendy M Grossman (November 2nd 2011)

Edward Bernays, considered to be the 'father of public relations,' wrote, "Those who manipulate the unseen mechanism of society constitute an invisible government which is the true ruling power of our country. We are governed, our minds are molded, our tastes formed, our ideas suggested, largely by men we have never heard of...in almost every act of our lives whether in the sphere of politics or business in our social conduct or our ethical thinking, we are dominated by the relatively small number of persons who understand the mental processes and social patterns of the masses. It is they who pull the wires that control the public mind, who harness old social forces and contrive new ways to bind and guide the world."[165]

He went on to admit, "Whatever of social importance is done today, whether in politics, finance, manufacture, agriculture, charity, education, or other fields, must be done with the help of propaganda. Propaganda is the executive arm of the invisible government."[166]

In America this is done through a combination of the centralization of media ownership and through secret government programs which work to influence the news and entertainment media. In

---

[165] Bernays, Edward – *Propaganda* page 37-38

[166] Bernays, Edward – *Propaganda* page 47-48

the 1970s a Senate investigation uncovered the CIA's media manipulation program called Operation Mockingbird, which was paying a billion dollars a year (in today's dollars adjusted for inflation) to the top editors and journalists of every major newspaper and television network to function as covert gatekeepers and propagandists for the government.[167]

The director of the program, Thomas Braden, would later admit, "If the director of the CIA wanted to extend a present, say, to someone... suppose he just thought, this man can use fifty thousand dollars, he's working well and doing a good job—he could hand it to him and never have to account to anybody...There was simply no limit to the money it could spend and no limit to the people it could hire and no limit to the activities it could decide were necessary to conduct the war—the secret war...It was multinational."[168]

According to the Congressional report into the matter, which was published in 1976, "The CIA currently maintains a network of several hundred

---

[167] Final Report of the Select Committee to Study Government Operations With Respect to Intelligence Activities. April 1976. pp. 191–201

[168] Thomas Braden, interview included in the Granada Television program, *World in Action: The Rise and Fall of the CIA* (1975)

individuals around the world who provide intelligence for the CIA and at times attempt to influence opinion through the use of covert propaganda. These individuals provide the CIA with direct access to a large number of newspapers and periodicals, scores of press services and news agencies, radio and television stations, commercial book publishers, and other foreign media outlets."[169]

Of course the CIA and top media figures deny such thing continues today—a claim which is absurd and demonstrably false. The Mockingbird program [or whatever codename it operates under today] keeps certain stories out of the news or at least prevents them from being a top story, and also functions to direct the news networks to highlight specific stories or cast them in a certain light. Top stories and issues stuck circling in the news cycle for days or weeks are often carefully chosen for specific purposes.

Even seemingly innocent entertainment is often covertly controlled and carefully crafted to function as propaganda. It's an open secret that the CIA and the Department of Defense have Entertainment Liaison Offices which work directly with Hollywood producers and writers to help

---

[169] Final Report of the Select Committee to Study Government Operations With Respect to Intelligence Activities (April 1976)

them make TV shows and blockbuster movies that deliver certain political messages in their story lines.[170]   Shows like *24* and films like *Zero Dark Thirty* were used to promote the idea that suspected terrorists need to be tortured in order to save people's lives, and that the heroes sometimes have to break the rules in order to save the day.[171]

These liaison offices also provide consultants, access to military bases which are used for shooting locations, expensive equipment like aircraft carriers, jets, tanks, etc., which are used in the projects, and even uniformed U.S. military soldiers who serve as extras.[172]   In exchange for this priceless equipment, large numbers of extras, and access to actual military bases; TV and film studios agree to turn over the final script approval to the entertain liaison officers who make changes in screenplays in order to mold them into

---

[170] *Army Times* "The Pentagon's Hollywood Liaison" by Hope Hodge (July 1 2013)

[171] *Variety* "The '24' Effect: How 'Liberal Hollywood' Carried Water For Torture" by Brian Lowry (December 14th 2014)

[172] *Business Insider* "One Man In The Department Of Defense Controls All Of Hollywood's Access To The Military" by Aly Weisman (March 5th 2014)

delivering the message they desire and have the final say over the plot.[173]

The emergence of social media has provided a problem for the dominant traditional media outlets, since they give anyone the ability to potentially have their message reach just as many people as content distributed through the mainstream media channels. While this has empowered the average person who can write a blog, post something on Facebook, or upload a video on YouTube and make it available for anyone to see, the corporate controllers have been scrambling to attempt to control this medium as well.

Facebook and Instagram can—and do—make content containing specific keywords, certain hashtags or pictures, disappear down the memory hole and the posts just don't show up on others feeds or in searches.[174] These services can prevent posts from going viral by limiting their distribution, largely without anyone detecting a

---

[173] *The Guardian* "An Offer They Couldn't Refuse" by Matthew Alford and Robbie Graham (November 13th 2008)

[174] *Gizmodo* "10 Normal Hashtags That Instagram Bans for Some Weird Reason" by Casey Chan (August 26th 2013)

post is being censored.[175] By using these popular social media and video sharing services, everyone must agree to their terms of service, which allow these companies to restrict free speech under the banner of what they deem "inappropriate."[176] People are locked out of accounts as punishment for several days or have their entire account shut down for "violating the terms of service" if they post something the companies have deemed violates their standards.[177]

By the time most of these major social media companies became widely used by the public, they were quietly purchased by massive corporations after being auctioned off at the secretive Sun Valley Conference which is held in Idaho every

---

[175] *Los Angeles Times* "Facebook tries to cut down on hoaxes showing up in news feeds" by Tracey Lien (January (20th 2015)

[176] *The Washington Post* "Two weeks after Zuckerberg said 'je suis Charlie,' Facebook begins censoring images of prophet Muhammad" by Caitlin Dewey (January 27th 2015)

[177] *Breitbart* "Facebook Plans to Crack Down on 'Hate Speech' Directed at Unspecified 'Protected Groups'" by John Hayward (March 16th 2015)

summer.[178] This small gathering in a remote town brings together the newest social media startups to meet with the current big names in technology, media, as well as heads of the CIA, NSA, and other government agencies where they come to a consensus on how to deal with new, independent communication companies and emerging technology.[179]

It's a Brave New World, and even though we're living in the Information Age, most people unfortunately couldn't care less about current events, history, or the direction society is headed. They instead have become lost in an entertainment wasteland and are constantly streaming digital distractions to occupy their mind with meaningless gibberish, crude comedy, and gratuitous violence in what many people now consider to be an Idiocracy or the Entertainment Age.

---

[178] *New York Times* "Business Casual" by David Carr (July 13th 2007)

[179] *Los Angeles Times* "Allen & Co.'s Sun Valley conference to focus on foreign affairs" by Joe Flint (July 10th 2012)

Conclusion

Is the press in America really free and independent when, for over 50 years, every major American newspaper and television network have buried their heads in the sand each year when the Bilderberg Group meets? Did they *all* just miss the story year after year, decade after decade? No news editor or journalist can honestly say the annual meeting isn't interesting and newsworthy. Certainly it can't be called a coincidence when word of Bilderberg began to go viral through social media and alternative news websites, that finally some mainstream outlets began mentioning it in passing—almost always, of course, pointing out that "conspiracy theorists" were suspicious.

Their tax returns show that media companies like the *Washington Post* have literally helped to pay for their meetings, and major talk radio show hosts who have their finger on the pulse of politics in America have either played dumb pretending to know nothing about Bilderberg, or ridiculed anyone asking reasonable questions about the group or their activities.

Perhaps now that they've been forced out of the shadows, Bilderberg will attempt to "go legit" and pretend the decades of denials, news blackouts, and ridicule of the "conspiracy theorists" who are curious or concerned about them just didn't happen at all. As we've seen countless times throughout history, after corrupt politicians and corporate leaders repeatedly dodge questions, deny facts, and ridicule inquiries—the truth of their activities eventually comes out.

Everyone knows that politics is a dirty business and lying is pretty much the only policy politicians are consistent on. They flip flop, they soften their positions in order to gain favor with certain groups and avoid offending others hoping to get elected, and if anyone knows anything about politicians and billionaire businessmen it's that they will do anything to gain and maintain their power. The list of massive deceptions perpetuated by those in power is long. "There are Weapons of Mass Destruction in Iraq." "The NSA isn't spying on American citizens." "If you like your health insurance policy, you can keep it." "Read my lips, no new taxes." And now we can add "the Bilderberg Group is just a conspiracy theory," to that list as well.

In 2011 when the digital dam began to burst, and the Drudge Report first posted about it, *Forbes* magazine finally decided to write an article which started off saying, "The annual Bilderberg Conference will convene this weekend, thus throwing the Internet into a tizzy," and that

"Conspiracy theorists believe the Bilderbergers control the course of world events. That through crisis and uncertainty they steer society's great developments with an ultimate goal of establishing a New World Order."[180]

After making the customary dig at "conspiracy theorists," the *Forbes* article surprising got somewhat serious, saying, "It is certainly concerning that representatives from Washington, Wall Street and the media will meet with no account of their dealings or details of their plans. Their counterparts from across the North Atlantic will attend too. It reeks of collusion and intrigue. The lack of transparency and potential for concentrated power spurs the imagination, while unsettling the mind. The media, despite some of its most influential personalities participating, will ignore the proceedings."[181]

That same week *Time* magazine also broke their silence, admitting, "In the past few years, the mystery surrounding the Bilderberg group has faded slightly because of interest from journalists," and as expected, added, "the

---

[180] *Forbes* "Bilderbergers, New World Orders And Conspiracy Theories" by Billa Flax (June 9th 2011)

[181] Ibid.

defenders of the 'conspiracy theory' who keep denouncing the 'Illuminati' are still active."[182]

Only time will tell what happens regarding the Bilderberg Group's secret history. You can't put the toothpaste back in the tube, as the saying goes, so I wrote this book as a record of the decades of denials and news blackouts of one of the world's biggest conspiracy *facts*.

Unfortunately most of their work is pretty much done. The New World Order global government is in its final phase; the Big Brother Orwellian surveillance systems have been built to track, trace, and database all electronic communications;[183] the American Constitution has been subverted; most of the population has been sedated, distracted, and dumbed down through endless entertainment available at the click of a mouse or the tap of a finger. But thankfully at the same time, the era of Bilderberg's secrecy is coming to an end, and for those who take the time

---

[182] *Time* "Bilderberg: The Uber-Powerful Global Elite Meet Behind Closed Doors in St. Moritz" by Anne Fournier (June 9th 2011)

[183] Checkout my previous book *Big Brother: The Orwellian Nightmare Come True* in paperback on Amazon.com or download the e-book to learn the details of electronic surveillance today and how our society parallels *George Orwell's Nineteen Eighty-Four.*

to research things for themselves instead of just consuming what the mainstream media is dishing out, a clear vision of reality can come into focus.

Thanks for reading this book to the very end. I hope you have found it concise and to the point without getting bogged down by unnecessary filler or unconfirmable wild accusations. I personally have been studying the Bilderberg Group for over ten years and it has been fascinating to see word spread so far and wide about them in the age of social media and YouTube.

If you found this book interesting or valuable in your pursuit of the truth please take a moment to write a brief review and rate it on Amazon.com or at the e-book store where you downloaded it from. And if you'd like to continue reading about similar subjects, I encourage you to download the e-book or order the paperback version of one or more of my other titles. They will save you countless years of research and have most of the esoteric pieces of the puzzle assembled and organized in in one place.

Thanks again for being a reader and a lover of books. It is certainly a dying pastime in our entertainment age, as we are on the verge of an apparent Idiocracy as society continues to sink down a cultural abyss. As media analyst Neil Postman wrote in his 1985 classic *Amusing Ourselves to Death*, "When a population becomes distracted by trivia, when cultural life is redefined as a perpetual round of entertainments, when serious public conversation becomes a form of baby-talk, when, in short, a people become an audience and their public business a vaudeville act, then a nation finds itself at risk; culture-death is a clear possibility."[184]

---

[184] Postman, Neil - Amusing Ourselves to Death page 155-156

About the Author

Mark Dice is a media analyst, author, and political activist who, in an entertaining and educational way, gets people to question our celebrity obsessed culture and the role the mainstream media and elite secret societies play in shaping our lives.

Mark's YouTube channel has received over 100 million views and his viral videos have been mentioned the Fox News Channel, CNN, the *Drudge Report*, *TMZ*, the *New York Daily News*, the *Washington Times,* and other media outlets around the world.

He has been featured on various television shows including the History Channel's *Decoded, America's Book of Secrets*, and *Ancient Aliens*; *Conspiracy Theory with Jesse Ventura, Secret Societies of Hollywood* on E! Channel, *America Declassified* on the Travel Channel, and is a frequent guest on *Coast to Coast AM*, *The Alex Jones Show*, and more.

Mark Dice is the author of several popular books on secret societies and conspiracies, including *The Illuminati: Facts & Fiction, Big Brother: The Orwellian Nightmare Come True, The New World Order, Facts & Fiction, The*

Resistance Manifesto, *Illuminati in the Music Industry*, and *Inside the Illuminati*, which are all available in paperback on Amazon.com or e-book on Kindle, iBooks, Nook or Google Play.

While much of Mark's work confirms the existence and continued operation of the Illuminati today, he is also dedicated to debunking conspiracy theories and hoaxes and separating the facts from the fiction; hence the "Facts & Fiction" subtitle for several of his books.

While having respect for all authentic religions and belief systems, Mark Dice is a Christian and holds a bachelor's degree in communication from California State University. He lives in San Diego, California.

He enjoys causing trouble for the New World Order, exposing corrupt scumbag politicians, and pointing out Big Brother's prying eyes. The term "fighting the New World Order" is used by Mark to describe some of his activities, and refers to his and others' resistance and opposition (*The Resistance*) to the overall system of political corruption, illegal wars, elite secret societies, mainstream media, Big Brother and privacy issues; as well as various economic and social issues. This Resistance involves self-improvement, self-sufficiency, personal responsibility and spiritual growth.

Connect with Mark on:

Facebook.com/MarkDice
Twitter.com/MarkDice.com
YouTube.com/MarkDice
Instagram.com/MarkDice
MarkDice.com

Printed in Great Britain
by Amazon

66286571R00081